60 simple Secrets

EVERY PASTOR SHOULD KNOW

Flagship church resources

from Group Publishing

Innovations From Leading Churches

Flagship Church Resources are your shortcut to innovative and effective leadership ideas. You'll find ideas for every area of church leadership including pastoral ministry, adult ministry, youth ministry, and children's ministry.

Flagship Church Resources are created by the leaders of thriving, dynamic, and trend-setting churches around the country. These nationally recognized teaching churches host regional leadership conferences and are respected by other pastors and church leaders because their approaches to ministry are so effective. These flagship church resources reveal the proven ideas, programs, and principles that these churches have put into practice.

Flagship Church Resources currently available:

- *Doing Life With God*

- *Doing Life With God 2*

- *The Visual Edge:*
  Compelling Video Connectors for Your Worship Experience

- *Mission-Driven Worship:*
  Helping Your Changing Church Celebrate God

- *An Unstoppable Force:*
  Daring to Become the Church God Had in Mind

- *A Follower's Life:*
  12 Group Studies on What It Means to Walk With Jesus

- *Leadership Essentials for Children's Ministry*

- *Keeping Your Head Above Water:*
  Refreshing Insights for Church Leadership

- *Seeing Beyond Church Walls:*
  Action Plans for Touching Your Community

- *unLearning Church:*
  Just When You Thought You Had Leadership All Figured Out!

With more to follow!

Dave Stone • Rick Rusaw

60 simple Secrets

EVERY PASTOR SHOULD KNOW

Flagship church resources
from Group Publishing

Dedication

This book is dedicated to our wives, Beth Stone and Diane Rusaw. Fortunately for us, we both learned early in our ministries that the *simplest secret* is to marry above yourself. Ladies, we did! Thanks for sharing your husbands with others and for being great moms, wives, and reflections of Christ in the fishbowl of ministry.

60 simple Secrets EVERY PASTOR SHOULD KNOW
Copyright © 2002 Dave Stone and Rick Rusaw

Visit our Web site: **www.grouppublishing.com**

Credits
Authors: Dave Stone and Rick Rusaw
Creative Development Editor: Paul Woods
Editor: Gary Wilde
Chief Creative Officer: Joani Schultz
Copy Editor: Alison Imbriaco
Art Director: Kari K. Monson
Computer Graphic Artist: Tracy K. Donaldson
Illustrator: Gary Locke
Cover Art Director: Jeff A. Storm
Cover Designer: Blukazoo Studio
Cover Illustrator: Gary Locke
Production Manager: Peggy Naylor

Unless otherwise noted, Scripture taken from the HOLY BIBLE, NEW INTERNATIONAL VERSION®. Copyright © 1973, 1978, 1984 by International Bible Society. Used by permission of Zondervan Publishing House. All rights reserved.

Library of Congress Cataloging-in-Publication Data
Stone, Dave, 1961-
    60 simple secrets every pastor should know / by Dave Stone and Rick Rusaw.
        p. cm.
    ISBN 0-7644-2345-2 (pbk. : alk. paper)

    1. Pastoral theology. I. Title: Sixty simply secrets every pastor should know. II. Rusaw, Rick, 1958- III. Title.
    BV4011.3 .S76 2002
    253--dc21

                                                                            2002002582

10 9 8 7 6 5 4 3 2 1   11 10 09 08 07 06 05 04 03 02
Printed in the United States of America.

Contents

Preaching and Teaching

Reaching Out

Timesaving and Efficiency

Professional Development

Introduction

You've probably seen the books *[Whatever the subject may be] for Dummies*. These are a wonderful collection of how-to books on a variety of subjects. They offer shortcuts, ideas, timesavers, and proven methods for doing your job better. If we were simply putting a book together for ourselves, then *Ministry for Dummies* would have been a perfect title. But *Ministry for Dummies* just didn't seem like a great marketing idea!

This is not a book about *why* we do ministry; it's about *how* we do it. In short, this is a book by dummies for those who are looking for practical ways to become more effective and efficient in ministry.

We do not consider ourselves experts in ministry and could easily supply names and addresses of people who would confirm that opinion. This book is a collection of observations and lessons learned from watching others and falling off our own bikes dozens of times over the last twenty years or so.

You've heard the story of the magician who seems to cut a woman in half in front of hundreds of onlookers. After the performance, he is asked by an astonished man, "Tell me how you did that?"

The talented magician whispers, "Can you keep a secret?"

The anxious man excitedly says, "Sure!"

The magician leans closer and says, "So can I."

Every profession has some tricks of the trade, shortcuts gleaned by those who have walked the road before. While some may choose to keep those secrets to themselves, we've chosen to share ours—an hour's worth of the *One-Minute Manager* for ministers. Sixty tips that will make ministers more effective.

Some of these secrets are actually not secrets at all. Some will be helpful, while others may be utterly useless to you in your situation. But if, ultimately, any of them assists one of us to be a little more effective, we will consider this a worthwhile effort.

The pressures mount; the demands increase. If ever there was a time ministers need practical advice, it's now. Whether you are just starting out or a seasoned veteran, you will want to put some of these principles into action immediately. Some will save you time; some ideas may point your church toward spiritual and numerical growth; others will help you serve people in a better way.

This book is written in response to co-laborers on this journey called ministry who have asked us, "How do you do it?"

And we have responded, "Can you keep a secret? Neither can we!"

Everyday Life in the Church

What's Next?

A simple Secret:
Be of value right where you are.

I had moved to Fort Myers, Florida, to begin my first ministry in a local church. I was a young man, and I was filled with aspirations, not only for this opportunity but for other places with other opportunities. It wasn't that I considered this church to be merely a steppingstone, something to endure until a better situation arose. No, it was a wonderful place with plenty of opportunity. But I also knew that those who do their ministries well are usually offered leadership positions involving larger venues: national ministries, statewide conventions, plum speaking engagements.

Ambition can be a good thing. But ambition coupled with immaturity can be disastrous.

Also on staff at this congregation was a semi-retired man who was nearly eighty years old. Dr. Lester Ford, former engineer, preacher, and college president, had moved to Florida to retire. There one of his "Timothys" asked him to help at the church. So, a few days a week, Dr. Ford gave his time, and he was particularly interested in taking me under his wing. I learned much from him that has served me well over the years, and I recall his friendship with great fondness. It was from Dr. Ford that I received the single best piece of advice I had ever heard.

One day at lunch he asked me, "What are your dreams for the future, Rick?" With plenty of enthusiasm, I shared the things that were on my heart. Dr. Ford listened carefully. He helped me shape some of my ideas, encouraged many, smiled at some, and simply laughed at others, as if somehow they were familiar to him. After we had spoken of the future at great length, he leaned across the table and said, "Rick, you have plenty of great dreams, and you should never stop dreaming. But along the way, learn to be of value where you are."

He told me I'd be of little value in the future if I didn't learn to give everything I had to what I was doing right then. He said simply, "Don't worry about being of value where you *aren't.*"

I meet plenty of ministers who spend a good deal of time talking about how things would be if they were in a different place. They long for a time everything will come together just right. That's when they will be valued and their abilities and capabilities will be realized. Longing for a better situation or dreaming of the future, they never realize their potential where they are.

Over the years I've had my own share of dreams and opportunities. And they have all been served by that simple piece of advice: Give the best effort, energy, passion, and prayer to what you are doing at the moment. Quit wondering what it might be like to be in another place, with different circumstances, or with different people. Stop spending the best part of your day focused on the would'ves, could'ves, and should'ves. Simply be of value where you are.

—RR

2 A Common "Mis-steak"

A simple Secret:
The devil's in the details—really!

s I left the steakhouse after a great meal, I hesitated in the lobby in search of a much-needed toothpick. Noticing my plight, the hostess said, "Sorry, sir. You know, I've been telling them they need to order more toothpicks."

Until that moment my dining experience had been great. But it was all undone by the last impression. I worried that lunch would be visible to every hospital patient I'd greet—unless I could extricate it with the corner of a business card and the aid of my car's rearview mirror.

To make matters worse, I had encountered the same problem at this steakhouse eight days earlier. I left with a bad taste in my mouth (not to mention between my teeth).

Lest you think this ministry secret belongs in the restaurant-review section of your newspaper, allow me to build the bridge. You see, the main goal of any restaurant is to provide quality food and service. Similarly, we in the church have some foundational goals. As someone has said, "The main thing is to keep the main thing the main thing." Successful churches and leaders excel in that regard. They craft an overall mission statement that provides a necessary compass for future direction.

But what about specific goals and standards for each minute area of ministry? With that kind of planning, you can constantly adjust your actions and modify your methods—even in the seemingly inconsequential areas of ministry—in order to accomplish your purposes in every situation.

Right down to the toothpicks.

I say that because I've seen some churches that remind me of my well-meaning steakhouse. They excel in first impressions, from a warm greeting at the front door all the way through to providing quality spiritual food in the worship service. But the details are overlooked. After a spiritual feast, worshippers may be faced with closing announcements that go on too long, inefficient nursery pickup methods, or poor traffic flow in the parking lot.

The worship service may have been great, but if critical details are unattended, the worshippers may leave with a bad taste in their mouths.

Why not begin by bringing your board members together to ponder questions such as these:

• Do visitors have a place to park and obtain more information about the church?

• Do parents feel comfortable and confident about the security and well-being of their children?

• Do seekers know where to go to meet the minister or to request prayer?

• Can people easily find out what your church believes?

If you take such important details for granted, your visitors' worship experience may fade in the "lobby." If your goal truly is excellence, then take the necessary steps to reach it—all the way from feasting on God's Word to providing those essential "ministry toothpicks." In other words, if the devil is going to bring you down, he'll probably do it by getting you to overlook all those little...you know.

—DS

Return to Sender

A simple Secret:
You can respond effectively to all those critics.

One of the least enjoyable aspects of ministry is receiving critical letters. You certainly don't enjoy being criticized, especially when you've poured yourself into preparing a message or program. One cynical remark can rock your world, if you let it. And those frustrating *anonymous* notes! Dwight L. Moody once received a letter consisting of a single word: "Fool!" Moody quickly responded with a public announcement: "This is the first time I've ever heard of anyone who signed his name and then forgot to write the letter."

Sometimes the best way to handle criticism is simply to maintain a sense of the ridiculous. In fact, you absolutely must maintain a sense of humor about some of the letters you receive, or you'll go crazy. The more far-fetched the criticism or outlandish the charge, the easier it is to laugh off. The toughest to handle are the critical words that do indeed contain some truth, perhaps requiring an apology and a change of behavior in the future. In these cases, the sooner the better is a good policy.

There are other things you can do, in addition to maintaining a sense of humor, to respond effectively to inevitable criticism. Here are my Top Ten suggestions:

1. Remain determined not to become defensive, and read the letter twice. Try to decipher the spirit of the writer, who may be struggling with legitimate anger.

2. In composing your response, look for even the smallest way to agree with the writer's points upfront.

3. Thank the individual for signing his or her name.

4. Commend the writer for coming directly to you and not talking behind your back to others.

5. Look for the truth in the criticism. Is some or all of it deserved or accurate?

6. If the letter is written with a gentle spirit, be certain to commend that—and respond in kind.

7. After writing your response, ask a couple of ministry cronies, secretaries, or other friends to tell you if it is too soft, too sharp, or just right.

8. Pray about what to change in the letter before sending it.

9. Make certain to close the letter with a positive comment such as, "Thanks for taking the time to share your concerns with me."

10. Always take the high road. Someone once said, "Never get in a contest of wills with a skunk. Even if you win, you'll still come out smelling bad."

Remember that the longer you're in ministry the easier it becomes to field criticism. Charles Swindoll wrote, "Maturity is moving from soft skin [and a] tough heart to tough skin [and a] soft heart." But it's always easier to accept constructive criticism from someone who has encouraged you in previous letters. When you receive that kind of mail, do express genuine thanks and appreciation.

(Note: If you disagree with my Top Ten and choose to write me a malicious letter, please have the decency to sign your name. And do me a favor—please enclose a self-addressed, stamped envelope. When you get as many critical letters as I do, the cost of postage stamps can eat you alive!)

—DS

4 Note to Self: What Did I Promise?

A simple Secret:
Note it on Sunday; do it on Monday (or Tuesday).

It's difficult to weather the information onslaught that hits us all at church on Sunday. Right in the midst of our responsibilities, well-intentioned individuals add to our To Do lists just when countless practical concerns—about services, music, sermons, teachers, visitors—are swirling around in our minds. No wonder it's hard to recall on Monday all the promises we made the day before.

Who can remember, for instance, to look up "the name of the book you quoted in your sermon last Groundhog Day"? For pastors, those moments before and after worship are a blur. Even so, we have an obligation to recall and meet the commitments we've made.

The solution: Make a note of it. One of the simplest ways to handle the barrage is to carry a 3x5 flip notebook. It fits in your pocket and can serve as an ongoing reminder of commitments from previous Sundays as well. However you do it, record your thoughts *in detail* on Sunday.

Here are a few more tips:

· Do not—I repeat—do *not* trust your memory. If you do, you run the risk of forgetting something important or missing a prime opportunity to minister. Don't forget: Your integrity is on the line.

· On Monday morning, review the promises you recorded, and attack them as early as possible. People are waiting to see what you will do.

· Transfer commitments to your day planner, and schedule time to handle them as soon as you can. The longer you wait to do what you said you'd do, the more those commitments will hang over your head.

· Delegate those responsibilities that are appropriate for your secretary or another assistant to handle.

· Keep a running record of the names of people you meet each week, and keep your list from week to week. The pad will be at your fingertips when you see these folks walking in from the parking lot and you need a quick refresher.

· Devote a section to prayer requests. For instance, if you're talking with a pregnant woman, you may ask the due date of the baby. After speaking with her, record that day in your flip pad. On Monday record a reminder on your calendar of the final weeks of the pregnancy so you can call her and let her know you are praying for her. (Then make certain you do pray for her that week.)

· For requests that require callbacks, give yourself a cushion. Say, "I'll try to call you on Monday or Tuesday." That way, if your schedule permits you to call on Monday, it will be a pleasant surprise for the church member.

If you want to improve your ability to manage all the information that comes your way each Sunday, remember this simple secret: Make detailed notes on Sunday, then follow through on Monday.

—DS

Lights, Camera, Action!

A simple Secret:
Prepare what you want to say when members of the media call.

If you're in the ministry for any length of time, chances are you'll eventually find yourself face to face with the media. Someday your secretary will inform you that a reporter is waiting on line 1 to hear all about the parsonage fire. Or that the cameras are on the way to film the raucous protestors in your parking lot.

You'll respond better on the spot if you understand how reporters work. Their job is to report a story, and stories are more interesting when there's drama, preferably created by some conflict. Responsible journalism requires reporters to get an opposing view—and that's often why they call you! At other times the story might focus on an event you have planned, so a reporter will find someone who takes issue with how you're going about it or why.

Since good media relations are desirable, here are a few tips that may help you make the most of the opportunity:

Accept the reporter's basic motivations. Understand that he or she wants a good, interesting story. Knowing that "just the facts" won't hold a reader's attention, you can help set the stage for dramatic tension in the story if you're ready to offer your slant on the matter. I've found that the easier you can make a reporter's job, the more likely he or she will be to include your view and tone.

Memorize written notes. Jot down and memorize key phrases that you hope will be included in the final story. When you answer questions, try to work these phrases into your answers several times throughout the interview. It doesn't hurt to keep repeating what is important to you.

Speak in sound bites. Concentrate on conveying complete ideas in short, verbal bursts. Choose your words carefully. In a perfect world, your words will not be changed, but "Dorothy, you're not in Kansas anymore."

Write down a few sentences that can be spoken in less than eight seconds. Anything longer will rarely be used in its entirety. Be aware that the line before or after may be cut. A half-hour interview by a newspaper journalist may be reduced to three quotes from you. A five-minute television interview will be edited into a two-sentence statement. It may be your best line; it may be your worst.

Smile, smile, smile. Observe a few television interviews and notice who smiles and who frowns. The reporter may believe that pastors are only stuffy, self-righteous, holier-than-thou types. Frowns feed that stereotype. On the other hand, smiles communicate the joy and love of the Lord.

Correct your mistakes immediately. If you aren't pleased with an answer or become tongue-tied, immediately put up your hand and say, "Let me try that again." Your hand motion will probably discourage the reporter from using that particular video footage. You can then say, "Let me answer that again; I know I can do better."

The reporter wants the best footage and comments he or she can get. Second and third takes are fine when your statements are more concise and more usable.

Build good relationships. The clergy often criticize the media. Why not try another approach? Take a personal interest in reporters' lives and problems. Send thank-you notes when they cover your events. If you're interviewed about a controversial issue and a reporter fairly presents your side, write to thank the reporter. Invite reporters to special events at your church—not so they can cover the event but because you're concerned about their spiritual health. Your job is to be salt and light to them, not to put them in their place.

Remember, too, that you can also build good will by volunteering your resources. Let reporters know that, when they need comments from a certain type of family or from a member of the community, they can call you for helpful sources. You can, in turn, use such opportunities to promote positive and Christlike values, as well as minister to local reporters.

—DS

The Minister's Family

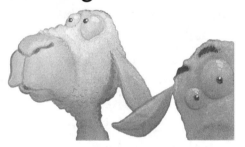

Vacation From Vocation: Enjoy!

A simple Secret:
You can vacation—and still preserve your vocational peace of mind.

Ministry can be quite taxing. A good vacation provides a mental escape and allows you to get physically energized and relationally recharged. Days off do more than help you catch your breath; vacations provide time to be refreshed by the special nurturing of your family and the Lord.

But it's important to begin your vacation with peace of mind. There's no sense heading off to the hinterlands harboring a sneaking suspicion that things will have "fallen apart" by the time you return. So let me offer a few simple tips that can keep your vocation from ruining your vacation.

• Schedule your vacation *after* a hectic stretch, not before it. Have you heard just-married couples say at the reception, "Just get me to the honeymoon"? Pulling off a big event at church can be extremely demanding, and ministers are constantly planning, preparing, and preaching at big events. Knowing you're scheduled to jump into a whirlwind of activity on the day you return will detract from your final days of vacation.

• Try to stagger your vacation time with that of other staff members. If your leadership team coordinates time away, church events will flow more smoothly. Scheduling in advance allows you to cover for others when they are gone, and vice versa. That way, everyone can enjoy time away without fretting.

• If possible, do get out of town. My worst vacations were at home as I tried to complete everything on my Honey Do list. That homebound "vacation" usually ends in frustration after it becomes common knowledge to your flock that you're still in town. You'll likely end up officiating at a funeral, making a couple of hospital visits, and hearing your family say a dozen times, "You seem preoccupied."

• Stay *reasonably* in contact—within set boundaries. My advice is simply to check your voice mail twice while you're gone. That's it. For example, if you'll be away from Saturday to Saturday, tell your secretary you'll check your voice mail on Tuesday night and Friday morning. This will give her the luxury of getting crucial questions answered while you're away. Give her your hotel phone number or cell number in case of an emergency. (The death of the church treasurer, for example, would be an emergency; the bulletin-folding machine breaking down is not.)

Finally, while you're sitting on a white, sandy beach, basking in the tropical sun or drinking mugs of hot chocolate in your mountain hideaway, don't forget the most important thing of all: *Pour yourself into your family.* Make every effort to concentrate on the ones you love the most. Leave your church problems at church. (Don't worry; they'll still be there when you return.) It's much better for your spouse and family to see you engrossed in them rather than stressed out by a church situation which, ultimately, is in God's hands anyway.

—DS

Change Those Lyrics!

A simple Secret:
Even in the ministry, you can enhance family life.

Recently my wife and I were asked to speak at a conference on parenting. It took us less than two nanoseconds to decline. We've decided to refrain from giving parental advice until our grandchildren turn out OK. We figure that may take awhile, as our three children are eighteen, sixteen, and eleven.

In fact, we're quite cautious about appearing to have all the answers on parenting. At times we have a wonderful relationship with our kids, and they seem to be developing quite well. At other times we wonder, *Wouldn't it have been easier to have cats?* (Except that I don't like cats.)

With two teenage boys and an eleven-year-old girl who thinks she's much older, we spend more time praying than we do sleeping. No one told me that, at this stage, the best noise I can hear at night is the sound of the garage door opening, preferably before curfew.

I have discovered that we ministers are not the only ones who struggle with maintaining healthy family relationships, but we definitely have the kind of vocation that can put pressure on the family. With that in mind, I asked some ministry friends what they do to enhance their family relationships, and here's what they told me:

Keep the marital romance alive. You've heard it said before, but it bears repeating because it's so crucial to family health: "The best thing you can do for your kids is to love your spouse." It's the first rule of successful parenting.

Preserve your day off. Work hard to keep this day off-limits to all but your family. It's easy to begin thinking that, because you're a minister, you ought to be always accessible. Not true! Obviously, emergencies do arise, and a few key people should know where to contact you. But guard your time off, and always include family members in planning your calendar. They'll appreciate the information and the input.

Plan a once-a-month special event with each child. Consider taking one of the kids to a ballgame, playground, dinner, movie—or anything that simply communicates how much you love and value that individual child.

Take your kids with you on trips. When you're speaking at or attending a meeting, take one of your children along, if possible. You can usually find ways to accommodate your child while you speak or attend a meeting, and the time you travel, stay in a hotel, and go out to eat together can pay huge dividends. Not only will you share an adventure, but your child will also have a chance to see you in action and realize that you're actually doing something besides just being gone!

Attend the kids' events. I'm amazed by the number of parents who are too busy to attend concerts, sporting events, or other activities their children are involved in. Your presence or lack of presence sends a clear message. Participate when you can; there isn't a town in America that isn't looking for parents to volunteer.

Eat your evening meal with your family. What better chance do you have for whole-family conversations, arguments, joke telling, conflict resolution, planning, and countless other interactions that just won't happen at any other time?

Don't use your kids as sermon illustrations. This advice may seem rather trivial, but it's a matter of building mutual trust—something quite important in a family. So unless you've asked permission first, find another story. (I realize some people may think they had children simply to provide great illustrations. As my kids have grown older, though, they have truly appreciated not being used in this way.)

Don't forget that eventually the kids will be out of the nest and you may long for the days when they wanted to spend time with you but you were too busy. When my boys were young, my job required lots of travel and lots of late nights away from home. I didn't realize the impact on my preschoolers until I heard one of them singing, "Jesus is my rock, and he rolls my blues away." However, my son had changed the words to "Jesus is my rock, and he rolls my daddy away." You can bet I tried to change those lyrics.

—RR

Family Priorities: You Make the Call

A simple Secret:
Getting your phone wet—a *good* thing.

I was on vacation, but I was not a happy camper. Standing on the dock, I looked down at cold, murky waters, twelve feet deep—under which lay my cell phone.

The phone had slipped from my hand, hit the dock, and bounced dramatically before sinking into the depths. For about an hour, several of us dove to the bottom, digging around in the muck, until we finally gave up and left for lunch.

My carelessness was going to cost me, and there was no one but me to blame. After lunch my brother-in-law suggested we give it another try. After

25

several unsuccessful dives, I told him it wasn't worth it because the phone would be ruined anyway. He said he was going to look one more time; then, amazingly enough, he emerged from the water with the phone.

Lake water streamed out of it, the display panel was full of tiny waves, and the buttons were caked with brown silt. But at least the phone had been found. After taking it apart and drying out the components, I attached the battery and, as expected, nothing happened. I had a dead phone and was in debt to my brother-in-law. It hadn't been a good day.

That night while I was tucking my eleven-year-old into bed, she said, "I'm glad you lost your phone; now you won't be talking on it all the time." I started to explain to her that I really wasn't on it *all* the time and some of those calls were absolutely necessary. But I heard her message: I had let the phone become more important to me than she was. (I really hate it when my eleven-year-old is wiser than I am.)

For the remainder of our vacation, I was phoneless. The world did not end, no major crises needed my intervention, and I didn't have to keep my kids waiting while I finished a call. In fact, I managed fine without my cell phone.

It's amazing to me how quickly we can allow our ministerial responsibilities to consume us. It isn't surprising that so many ministers have assumed that because they're needed they are indispensable or that the world might just end if they don't weigh in with their opinions.

My daughter was hearing from me that my "business" was more important than our vacation. Other folks were more valuable because they had my ear. Serving God meant having time for everyone but my family. So I was called to do a little self-evaluation.

As Paul Harvey says, "Now, the rest of the story..." Just as we were leaving for home, I picked up my cell phone and, as a joke, pushed the power button. It came to life and has worked fine ever since. (Should I shoot a commercial for the company?) But I learned that, as much as I need my phone for some things, I need to throw it in the lake once in a while too.

—RR

Family Ties

A simple Secret:
God first, family second, ministry third.

Juggling ministry and family time can be one of a pastor's greatest challenges. Since it seems your job is never done, your church responsibilities can frustrate the faith of your family members. To be loved by hundreds of church members is a hollow feeling if it isn't accompanied by the respect of those who know you best.

Your family should come in second place, right behind your relationship with the Lord. The only way that can become a reality is through consistent effort and a lot of prayer—along with four critical rules for every ministerial family.

Communicate orally. Your spouse and children need to hear from your lips that they are more important than your ministry responsibilities. Throughout the Bible, we are told to encourage one another. Who better to lift up with our words than those closest to us? Go out of your way to say the words they need to hear. The right words differ for each family member, but the closer you get to family members, the more you will know what each needs and wants to hear. Don't keep them waiting.

Schedule wisely. Your family needs to see in your schedule that you are willing to go to great lengths to protect your time together. Don't try to convince yourself that it is the *quality* of the time and not the *quantity* of time that's important. In reality it is both. I have a friend who designates before the beginning of the year the number of nights he will be away from home. He places that number of marbles in a jar, and then he removes one each night he is gone. When the marbles are gone, he stays home! Look for opportunities to establish family traditions, and block those times out in your day planner as early as you can. Get sports schedules, school dates, and other special events on your personal calendar as early as possible.

Be there constantly. Your goal is unlimited accessibility. Your family members must know in their hearts that they can get to you whenever they need to. That assurance brings relief and confidence. A spouse or child who continually sees that hundreds of church members seem to have direct access to you must be convinced that church members have more opportunities to receive your undivided attention. If family members don't feel you are available for them, they will soon stop trying to get your attention and will seek attention from other sources.

Develop your romantic side. Keep growing in your ability to love and respect your spouse. As Rick stated earlier, the best way to be a good father is to be a good husband. What a great principle to live by! If you treat your wife with love and respect, your children will be more apt to respect you as well.

Someone has pointed out that Noah preached for 120 years and yet he only saved seven people. But Noah accomplished something that many will not—he did save his entire family.

—DS

10 Why Not Include Them?

A simple Secret:
Win the "Family Versus Ministry" challenge!

L et's face it. The ministry can create a tug of war between time with family and time with church. Why not win this time challenge and involve your family in your ministry?

I'm not talking about the times you force your children to set up chairs for a banquet or fold bulletins. It's through experiences like those that your children may develop a negative impression of the church—and you! What I do suggest is looking for ways to have them participate on your turf in a positive way so that you'll all enjoy the benefits of time spent together for years to come. Begin by trying one or more of these ideas:

• Take one of your children with you when you visit or speak at another church. You'll expose your children to different styles of worship and foster good discussion as you drive home.

· Express special appreciation to your spouse. October is Clergy Appreciation Month (no doubt a scheme fueled by a greeting-card marketing executive married to a pastor). Why not choose a day in October to write your wife a note, letting her know you couldn't do it without her? Remind her that she is the wind beneath your wings.

· You've got a master key to the church; use it! Establish some traditions at the church building, apart from spending time at services. On Christmas afternoon, I take the kids to the church campus which, of course, is a ghost town on that day. We take scooters and have races in the fellowship hall or take golf balls and putters and make our own course in the hallways. Or we may go there one evening and play Hide-and-Seek in the dark. As strange as it may sound, it helps the kids see the place where Dad works as fun rather than as a place that only steals his time.

· Include your children in gifts you receive. On our tenth anniversary with our church, our members gave us a night at a nice downtown hotel. My wife and I told the kids that since they were such a big part of my ministry we wanted them to go with us. So we crammed all five of us into the hotel room. It worked out great, and it also assured them that they were appreciated, as well, for sharing their dad and being supportive of his ministry.

· Take your spouse or a child with you on a hospital call. The patient will be more excited about the visit, and you'll expose your family member to the hurts you see every day at work.

· Allow your kids to sift through the lost-and-found box. When we were growing up, my father allowed my brother and me to do that. Any item that had remained in the box for more than two months became fair game. Church took on a whole new meaning to this six-year-old who prayed diligently that no church member would come and claim the colored-pencil set dropped in the parking lot or the baseball magazine found in the back pew behind a church hymnal.

Everyone wins if you involve your family in your ministry. When you view your efforts at church as fulfilling and rewarding, then your family members will begin to feel the same way.

—DS

Pastoral Care

11 What's in a Name?

A simple Secret:
Remember a name; value a person.

A pastor had a clever way of making people think he remembered their names. The method served him well until the day he shook hands with a stately, elderly woman as she left the worship service. The preacher said, "Now help me out. Do you spell your last name with an 'i' or an 'e' "? The woman scowled and said, "With an 'i'...H-i-l-l."

Sometimes our efforts to remember do backfire. On the other hand, remembering someone's name is one of the greatest compliments we ministers can offer; it means we went the extra mile, even in a brand-new relationship, as busy as we are. The person thinks, *I've only been there three times; he meets so many people every day—and he remembered me!*

The question is, how much time and effort are you willing to invest in order to make people feel valuable in this way? Remembering names isn't as much a talent as it is a learned skill. Remembering names is like exercising a muscle: The more you use it, the stronger you get. Here are three steps that can get you started:

Repeat the name when you meet someone new. Say it aloud again before the conversation concludes. This confirms the pronunciation and allows you to hear the name again, which helps your retention.

Record the name so you can find it when you need it. Place it in a file folder, in a pocket-sized notepad, or in a document on your computer or Palm Pilot. The key is to have a designated place where you go to find names when you need them. Always include a brief descriptive phrase beside a new name, such as "brown hair Brenda" or "tall Paul." Make a game of it; test yourself on your way home.

Review the names on a regular basis. This is important, because short-term memory is passed on to long-term memory through review. It's how you can still remember words to songs that you haven't heard since you were a junior camper. You might do this review each Sunday morning before you head to church. That way, the names of people you met during the previous weeks will be fresh in your mind.

Whatever works for you is great, but there's no substitute for having some kind of method. My simple philosophy is: repeating + recording + reviewing = retention.

Tuck a few successes under your belt, and people's astonishment and appreciation will fuel your efforts. Just keep in mind that when people are choosing a church, they are looking for the personal touch. If God knows the number of hairs on our heads, the least we can do is call Mrs. Hill by name.

—DS

Being Christ in Crises

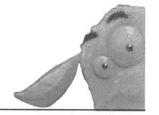

A simple Secret:
When tragedies arise, opportunities ensue.

I've heard many preachers refer to what James 1:2 teaches—and what it doesn't. Usually they point out that the verse doesn't say, "*If* you face trials"; it says, "*Whenever* you face trials" (italics added for emphasis). In other words, you can expect trials, big and small. Some trials affect only a family or a small group, while others, like the terrorist attacks of September 11, 2001, can shake the foundation of a nation.

Have you ever noticed that, when tragedy strikes, society's spotlight often focuses on the church rather than the American Civil Liberties Union? And since times of crisis move people to listen to what churches have to offer and what ministers have to say, be prepared to respond. In practical terms, you'll experience it this way: The church membership calls, wanting to organize volunteers; the media calls, wanting a statement or some words of comfort; the community calls, wanting some kind of service that can bring meaning to the madness. When crisis demands your attention, how do you and your church respond?

School shootings, drunk-driving accidents, attacks by terrorists, tornadoes, fires, and earthquakes compel our churches to serve as a conscience in the community. And we must also respond on the community's behalf. Sometimes the situation requires responding in a specific manner. At other times, the wisest course is to sit on the sidelines. In either case, we'll usually need to make quick decisions, such as changing the topic for the Sunday sermon at the last second or quickly publicizing a prayer service for the evening.

The response may be as small as including a specific line on the sign in the church's front yard. Or an appropriate response might require hours of planning and coordination. You may choose to offer a special service or set up a special fund for financial gifts to meet the needs of hurting or needy people.

The key is to remember that, when tragedies occur, opportunities arise for people to consider Christianity and look upward for help. We are to make "the most of every opportunity, because the days are evil" (Ephesians 5:16). In times of turmoil, speaking and acting with the right spirit is not taking advantage of an unfortunate situation. As Billy Graham once said, "The same sun that melts the butter also hardens the clay." In the face of extreme adversity, some hearts will turn hard and blame God. Other hearts will soften and turn to him as their source of strength.

In times of heartache, those who enter your church come in search of something eternally essential. Don't disappoint them. Lead them gently to God's Word where, in the midst of their pain and uncertainty, they can find both a comfort and a challenge.

—DS

Healthy Hospital Ministry

A simple Secret:
Every patient can be visited—every day.

O ne of our pastoral care team members was visiting an older church member in the hospital. She wanted to know when the pastor himself was coming to visit. Why hadn't she seen him yet? The visitor's response: "Ma'am, you don't want to be *that* sick." It would be wonderful if no one in your congregation ever became seriously ill. But we know better. And since our people are going to land in the hospital, we need to view those occasions as opportunities for ministry.

On the other hand, we rarely have the time to spend hours in the hospital on a regular basis. For a long time, our church didn't have enough staff members to cover hospital calls on a daily basis until I was able to enlist a number of volunteers with the requisite compassionate hearts. Now we get the job done. In fact, last week we had thirty-two people in various local hospitals. To the best of my knowledge, every patient was visited every day. Here are four things we attempt to achieve in hospital ministry.

First, we make sure someone is there to pray with the patient and family before any surgery or major procedure. We don't spend a great deal of time, especially when medical personnel are arriving to prepare the patient. I've often invited the doctor or nurse to join us, always leaving that person a graceful way out: "I know you are busy, but would you like to pray with us?" Many doctors and nurses are happy to join us.

Second, if the surgery is significant, we make sure that someone knows how to reach us if there's an emergency. If a family member would otherwise be alone, we have some folks who will come to the hospital and stay with him or her.

Third, after the surgery, we follow up with the family and patient and again, if possible, offer a brief prayer.

Fourth, we maintain an ongoing, organized ministry. Each day of the week is assigned to a staff person to ensure that needed visits are made in area hospitals. On Sundays, a team of volunteers takes the Lord's Supper and devotional material to the hospitals. The volunteers who work to make our hospital ministry possible receive training in the following do's and don'ts to ensure that their visits are meaningful:

· *Do* make sure you know the patient's name before you enter his or her room.

· *Don't* just barge into the room. If the door is closed, knock first. If the patient is sleeping, leave a note saying you were there.

· *Do* show respect to medical personnel who are performing their duties when you arrive. Wait for them to finish; they won't mind seeing you come in the future. When you're compassionate, considerate, and courteous, you are welcomed by the hospital staff. (I am amazed by the number of ministers who are perceived by hospital staff as arrogant or uncaring because of overbearing "bedside manners.")

· *Don't* give medical advice. Your job is to provide pastoral care, not to diagnose illness.

· *Do* take your coat off or pull up a chair and sit alongside the bed. Even if you are able to stay only a few minutes, it will seem as if you've been there longer. Of course, you don't have to spend hours to have a meaningful visit. Most people are grateful for any length of time you can spend with them.

· *Don't* forget to ask about the patient's prayer concerns—you can't *assume* you know what they are. When you need to leave, simply ask if it would be all right to pray together. Then take some moments to hear what's on the patient's heart.

As our program developed, we discovered that we could give sufficient attention to people while they were in the hospital but very little after they returned home. So we organized an after-care program, in which volunteers follow up with the patient on the phone after the patient is discharged. If possible, these volunteers also visit the person at home after a hospital stay. If there are special needs—providing transportation, picking up prescriptions, delivering meals, assisting with child care—the volunteers try to find a way to meet those needs. And when it comes to hospital ministry, that's the key: Keep seeking to meet the needs.

—RR

In the Time of Sorrow

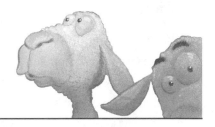

A simple Secret:
In funeral ministry, be yourself and let God use you.

We can provide comfort and guidance during the trying time of a loved one's passing. Here are four practical suggestions for making a service more meaningful and giving you the best chance at effective funeral ministry.

1. Let the funeral home handle the technical details. The funeral director can do a much more efficient job, and letting the funeral director know that he or she is responsible for the details will eliminate any possible misunderstandings. I once observed a situation in which both the funeral director and the minister thought the other had arranged for special music; unfortunately, neither had. Having no music for the service created additional stress for everyone. As soon as possible, meet with the funeral director to make sure you're both on the same page.

2. Arrange a time to meet with the family. Encourage family members to invite whomever they would like to attend. Remember, your job is to assist the family in planning the service. The person who was the closest to the deceased should have the most say about what is included. Often friends, neighbors, and relatives—though well-meaning—can give too much input, and you'll need to provide direction at the pre-funeral planning time. Here are some specific tips for that meeting:

· Begin with prayer and any brief words of comfort you may have for the family.

· Talk about the deceased. Ask the family and friends to tell you about the person who has died. The information they share will help you talk about personal attributes during the service. Be warned, though: Don't pretend that you knew the person if you didn't!

• Review the service. Agree on the time and place, and ask about viewings, a reception, and catering. Ask family members if they would like the service to include music, Scripture, readings, or eulogies. Be prepared to guide them through these decisions and offer suggestions when appropriate. (Note: If for some reason you do a number of funerals, make sure you change your service or message outlines so people don't assume that one size fits all.)

• Ask about participants. Often the family will want a friend or family member to speak; make sure you touch base with the individual ahead of time. Offer specific guidance as to time, appropriate things to say, and what to do if he or she becomes too emotional to continue. (I often recommend that potential speakers simply write something for me to read on their behalf.)

• Discuss including a visual presentation. More and more people desire video or PowerPoint presentations of their loved one during services. Encourage a limit on time (five minutes can be a long time, and ten can seem like eternity, making for an awkward service). Let the funeral director manage this presentation, but make sure you and the funeral director view and test the video prior to the service. Don't spoil the service with technical glitches.

3. Let God be the judge. Remember that nothing you say will get the deceased into heaven or keep him or her out. God and the deceased have worked that one out already. One man, who was planning services for his brother, asked the minister to say that his brother was a saint. The minister responded, "That will be tough. Everyone in town knows you and your brother were the most dishonest businessmen around. Everyone knows your brother cheated on his wife, was horrible to his kids, and manipulated everyone he could."

"I know," the brother replied. "But I'll give you twenty-five thousand dollars if you'll say he was a saint."

The service began, and the minister said, "You all knew Bob, and you know what a horrible man he was. You know all the despicable things he did, and you know there wasn't a decent bone in his body. But...compared to his brother, Bob was a saint."

4. Express your own emotions. If you were close to the deceased person, there's no need to stifle your grief. In fact, your own genuine emotion can be of great comfort to other mourners. However, contrived emotion can be a disaster for you and them.

In any case, do communicate in your message that we have a God of hope, challenge, and resurrection. Remember that people are looking to you for comfort. Hug, share a Scripture verse, engage mourners at their point of need—whatever allows you to come alongside them in their time of sorrow.

—RR

15 Counseling: Have You Thought It Through?

A simple Secret:
Wise pastors are ready to counsel—or not.

My six-year-old son, Samuel, was quite proud of the lizard he'd caught at the lake. But the next day, before heading to church, the Stone family made the mistake of putting the little creature in a glass container and leaving it outside. When we returned in the afternoon, the summer heat had fried the poor fellow.

As you can imagine, Samuel took the death hard. He pulled out the dead lizard and began to sob. He got a shovel and buried him in the mulch, placing a cross and a stone on the grave, then slipped away to cry some more.

About two hours later, Samuel was carrying something around on his tennis racquet and had a big smile on his face. *Good,* I thought. *He's found a new creature that's helping him work through his grief.* Then I learned he'd dug up the lizard and was showing off the corpse to neighbors. I said, "You can't do that; you've got to get rid of him out in the field."

Samuel came back a few minutes later and said, "Dad, it was so cool! I put him on my racquet and swung like a tennis player. I knocked him way out in the field!"

What a progression—from agony to Agassi in just a couple of hours.

In ministry you have probably learned that most of life's transitions don't occur quite so quickly and easily. When is it right to put on the hat of counseling? The answer will vary depending on the size of the congregation you serve, your giftedness, and the skills of your other staff and lay leaders. In any case, you've got to think through your approach upfront, and you've got to be sure of your abilities and your limitations. As you determine the scope of your role, consider these practical tips:

Refer when possible or prudent. Some situations will be out of your league and should immediately be referred to other professionals, such as psychologists or psychiatrists. Become acquainted with any local Christian counselors, as well.

Form support groups within your church or area. Support groups allow people in need to lean on others who share a common pain—dealing with grief, for example. Several people who are at different points in the healing process can often do much more to help than you can do in individual counseling.

Set the number of counseling appointments you will take each week. If counseling is a passion, and your schedule permits, you may allow six time slots to be earmarked for this ministry. Others may limit counseling appointments to one or two, depending on their situations.

Establish definite parameters. Be clear about the number of times you will meet with an individual or couple. Help folks understand that neither your available time nor your training will allow you to provide long-term personal counseling. Stick to one evening a week, for instance. Whatever you decide, realize that those boundaries will be stretched and tested frequently.

Guard your purity and reputation. If you are counseling a person of the opposite sex, it may be wise to keep the door open a little if there is no window between your office and the reception area. Always make certain there is a secretary or another person outside your office if you counsel during off hours. These safeguards can protect you from being tempted and from being falsely accused.

Utilize your church members. Most Type-A ministers prefer the Lone Ranger method. They work solo. But they also burn out. Be wise and make use of the body of Christ. Encourage volunteers within the church to exercise their gifts in showing mercy, discernment, and short-term directive counseling. For example, when a member of your congregation has a miscarriage, who better to minister than another woman who has experienced that tragedy and is healthily working through it?

I like the way the Apostle Paul referred to our God of comfort "who comforts us in all our troubles, so that we can comfort those in any trouble with the comfort we ourselves have received from God" (2 Corinthians 1:3-4). There will always be hurting people for Christian leaders to counsel. One of the best things we can do is to help them turn their focus from themselves to others—from sobbing to serving.

—DS

What *Not* to Say at a Funeral

A simple Secret:
You can concentrate on the positive—
and still remain faithful to Scripture.

Throughout my ministry, I've tried to be careful not to give false hope or mislead those who attend the funerals of their friends or family members. But on at least one occasion, due to the emotion of the moment, I stretched my theology beyond its limits. What I vowed I would never do with people, I did with horses. In January of 1995, a prestigious Kentucky horse barn caught fire, and eighteen Thoroughbreds died.

I was asked to speak at a memorial service at the horses' burial site, and several folks had convinced me that this was a prime opportunity to minister to people and expose them to Christianity. It turned out to be a high-profile outdoor service with dozens of people crying throughout my talk. In addition, several television news stations were on hand, getting it all on tape.

The grief response was more powerful than I had witnessed in most funeral services. I felt pretty good about the comfort I had given—that is, until I watched the local evening news. The lead story on the memorial service opened with the reporter saying, "Reverend Stone brought comfort to the mourning owners and their families by assuring them that they would be able to see their horses again in heaven someday."

Ouch! What sounded good before a grieving group no longer sounded biblically correct. Even though I found some pretty good supporting evidence for my statement, my clergy friends teased me for months. Even those with the gift of mercy called to ask if I could do a funeral for their goldfish—and then laughed hysterically before they hung up the phone.

I learned my lesson. In my zeal to encourage, I must remain faithful to the intent of the Scriptures. Eternal destiny is up to God.

Of course, it's true that we must walk a fine line at some funerals, especially when we're in doubt about the deceased one's salvation. But these suggestions may help you keep your balance:

• If the person obviously had no faith or relationship with the Lord, you will lose credibility if you paint a syrupy picture implying that all is well and that he or she is in heaven. Instead, concentrate on the person's good attributes. If Bill was generous, talk about what a godly characteristic generosity is ("For God so loved the world that he gave..."). If Sue was a servant, then tell how she served and then talk about Jesus washing the feet of the disciples.

• Share comforting Scriptures for the bereaved, but when you talk about the promises of heaven found in God's Word, make certain you don't specifically attach them to the unbeliever whom you are eulogizing.

• Remember, though, that the deceased may have had a faith in God that you did not know about. Have family members of the deceased tell you when the person made a commitment to the Lord. Ask them to recall some of the ways that his or her belief in Christ was reflected in everyday life.

Whether the funeral is for people or horses, try not to cross the ethical line of assigning them to heaven if you can't back it up with the Bible. Choice, not chance, will determine their eternal destination.

—DS

Preaching
and Teaching

Ready for Prime Time?

> ## A simple Secret:
> Sermons aren't ready until they're readily relevant.

So what? Every week there are people all over the world who leave a church service with these words ringing in their heads. *So what?* It's the same question I ask each week when I look at my sermon notes, believing the preparation part of my message is completed.

Do you, too, ask the question often? Will the message you've prayed and agonized over answer the "So what?" question? Will you offer a word of hope, challenge, truth, love, conviction, or encouragement? A practical word your people can take to their homes, their neighborhoods, their schools, and their places of employment?

We have a responsibility to take the gospel that never changes to a world that will never be the same. Can we communicate that message in a way that makes a difference in those who hear it? Or will they leave saying, "That was nice, but so what?"

> *Preach the Word, brother, preach it.*
> *Preach it high where men can teach it.*
> *Preach it low where men can reach it.*
> *But preach the Word, brother, preach it.*
> —*author unknown*

I hope at least three things will happen in our services each weekend: that people will *have a good time* (because they come to church convinced they're going to be unhappy), that they will *receive some hope* (because so much of their week is consumed with things that steal their hope), and that they will *feel challenged to change their lives* (because they're often stuck in habits and routines that seem unbreakable).

Our messages can accomplish these things only if we're putting a lot of thought into practical applications and immersing ourselves in the lives our hearers actually live, not just brushing up on a few new presentation techniques.

A few years ago, I was teaching in Austria. Not far from the small campus was a monastery with a small café, and I used to walk there for breakfast before classes. The first morning, I found that the young woman behind the counter spoke no English, which made it difficult to order my Danish roll and orange juice. So I did what comes naturally: I spoke louder and made sweeping gestures.

I received minimal results.

Fortunately for both of us, another customer intervened and placed my order. Unfortunately for me, I ate cheese Danish and orange juice every morning for six days. The counter lady would see me coming and, with a polite smile, give me my food. "*Danka*," I would gratefully reply.

It doesn't do us any good to shout the message or to become more animated if we haven't learned to speak the language. No matter how logical and well-organized our message, no matter how biblically sound it is, we aren't finished preparing until we can clearly answer the question "So what?"

—RR

Keep That Heart Beating!

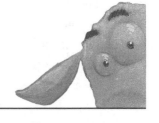

A simple Secret:
If you can't say it in a minute, you're not ready to preach it.

One of the best things I ever did to improve my preaching was also one of the most difficult. I took the tapes of my sermons and sent them to a small group of people who had agreed to critique my efforts. (As I shared this with our congregation, I told them there were a number of people who apparently *thought* they were in that group!) Over the years, I have continued this practice. At my request, the people in this group receive the tapes and provide their critiques.

I have asked them to be honest with their advice, and I've promised not to hold it against them. The groups have included ministers, professional speakers, drama teachers, regular folks, Christians and non-Christians. They've been extremely helpful. I am convinced there is no greater privilege than speaking the message of God. With that privilege comes a tremendous responsibility, because it would be a shame to deliver the greatest message of all time in a way that's hard to understand.

So, before the critique stage, what can we do to improve our speaking ability? I wouldn't presume to instruct you on how to craft the sermon, and besides, there are all kinds of wonderful resources to assist you with the textual-preparation aspect of preaching. (In this regard, remember that, according to Franklin P. Jones, "Originality is the art of concealing your source.") The point is: However you prepare, prepare well. That's half the battle.

But what about the other half—the actual delivery? I am amazed we don't concern ourselves more with developing our speaking skills. If we have gone to the trouble of preparing a sermon that puts God's message into a logical, well-illustrated outline, why do we assume that the work is done?

Some people are naturally gifted speakers, but all of us can improve our skills. Here's one simple method, in the form of a request that I often make of preachers looking for help: "Tell me in one minute what you're trying to tell the congregation in twenty or more." If you can boil your message down to one minute and still clearly communicate its essence, you can use the other minutes to clarify, illustrate, and expand. If you cannot clearly communicate the heart of the message in a minute, you will have trouble communicating it no matter how many minutes you have.

I encourage young ministers to take that one idea, that one thread, and weave it throughout the message. Sometimes it will be highly visible—and other times more subtle—but don't lose the thread. Know the heart of your message, and keep it beating throughout the sermon.

—RR

Oblivious to the Obvious

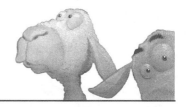

A simple Secret:
When "sharing some words," use the Word.

Y ou search, surf, and sift for stories and illustrations to improve your communication with your congregation. In your never-ending quest for good material to share with your people, let me suggest a good book I read recently: the Bible. I understand it's a bestseller each year. When I was in Bible college, my preaching professor spoke of where the power in preaching could be found. He taught us to locate it in a simple phrase found throughout the Scriptures: "Thus saith the Lord."

The Holy Spirit penetrates the hearts of listeners through the Word, not necessarily through clever quotes or humorous anecdotes about your mother-in-law. It is not even the awesome, amazing, and alluring alliterations you force into your outlines. The power for your lessons and sermons comes from the message of God revealed in the Word of God.

Of course, the Holy Spirit uses your unique personality and creativity to set the stage, as a kind of opening act. But God's Word is to be the main show, and we're assured that it will always accomplish its purposes (see Isaiah 55:11). So it only stands to reason that to *convey* God's Word we must *include* God's Word. And when it comes to quoting Scriptures to drive home a point, it's not a pinch here or a dash there; rather, it's like putting salt on watermelon in the summer. Don't use the salt sparingly; coat your message generously.

Just make certain your "Thus saith the Lord" is said in love rather than in judgment. Years ago I heard one of my favorite preachers, Olin Hay, describe his first sermon, preached when he was a teenager. He said, "I thought I had done pretty well. I'd really come down hard on the congregation and was quite proud of my scolding. But after the message, I asked my pastor how I did. He replied, 'Olin, you can't preach the love of God with a clenched fist.'" In the hands of a Christian leader, the Bible is to be used as a tool and not as a weapon. By its very nature, the Word can cut to the heart of us humans, to teach, rebuke, correct, train, and equip. Thus Ozark Christian College, in Joplin, Missouri, proclaims this motto: "The Word of Christ taught in the Spirit of Christ."

The Bible is filled with quotes of wisdom, stories of passion and faith, and down-to-earth examples to convey God's message to human hearts. So as you search for just the right story to drive home the point, don't neglect the resource that can make the biggest difference in your life and in the lives of your hearers—the Bible.

—DS

20 Connect the Dots of Your Thoughts

A simple Secret:
Good transitions make heavy-hitting sermons.

Recently I saw a baseball player drill one down the left-field line. The ball then caromed around in the corner. The unusual bounce made it obvious to the fans that what appeared at first to be a stand-up double would most likely become a triple. But then something happened. As this agile, professional athlete rounded second, he tripped on the base and sprawled on the dirt. He spent the next few seconds turning around and frantically crawling back to second base—barely ahead of the left-fielder's one-hop throw.

Sadly, such "turn around" situations aren't limited to the baseball diamond. Ill-prepared preachers have a knack for turning oratorical triples into doubles. In their preparation and delivery, they tend to concentrate more on the sensational story than on their transition out of it. The focus becomes the emotional conclusion, the hilarious joke, or the personal story, and little attention goes to the thematic bridge to the real point. If the material isn't masterfully connected, it becomes merely a collection of stories. While the crack of the bat and the slide in to home plate are dramatic, mastering the mechanics of running the bases is essential to the success of any hitter. A well-conceived transition following a story actually improves the story and takes it from good to great.

It's tough to measure the impact of a cohesive sermon versus that of a disorganized one. But your listeners know it when they hear it. Here's an example of a good story with a good transition:

A man attending the Special Olympics for the first time sat in the bleachers and watched seven learning-disabled kids compete in the hundred-yard dash. When the starter's gun sounded, all he saw were arms and legs flying every which way. But about halfway through the race, the boy who was in the lead suddenly tripped and fell to the ground. The spectator said he then watched an amazing thing happen. The other runners stopped running. They walked back. They picked the boy up and brushed him off. And then, arm in arm, all seven of them walked across the finish line together.

Transition sentence: And some people say they're not as smart as we are!

Do you see my point? The story itself is excellent. But the way we come out of it can elevate the quality and impact of the illustration. Investing the time to develop powerful transitions can move our illustrations from second base to home plate. It can even move good preaching into the realm of great preaching. If we'll go to the extra effort of linking our thoughts, we'll find that making these connections helps our listeners make life-changing commitments.

—DS

The Highlight of Your Sermon

A simple Secret:
If you can color it, you can remember it.

O ral communicators love to find the winning technique that can enhance their delivery. The president has his teleprompter. The news anchor has a live feed in her ear so she can sound as sharp as she looks. What is your technique as you stand in the pulpit each week? You know that part of striving for excellence is polishing the way you speak. The longer you teach and preach, the more you seek methods that can give your lessons an edge or a boost.

I've worked out a color-coding system by highlighting my manuscripts with magic markers. For example, I mark outline headings in green, key words in orange, Scripture in blue, humor in pink, serious illustrations in purple. Usually I circle each paragraph with the designated color.

The choice of colors isn't important as long as you consistently use the same ones to designate the same things. And you'll love the benefits of using this simple method. Color highlighting will help you...

improve eye contact. I select key words throughout the manuscript to help guide me as I tell the story. I highlight them in orange. This allows me to glance at my notes for shorter periods of time, which enhances my eye contact with the congregation and increases the impact of what I'm sharing.

find your next point quickly. If you're accustomed to reading your outline or manuscript a couple of times before you deliver your sermon, then the colors will help you even more. Your eyes won't need to frantically scour the page in search of your next phrase. You will know where to look.

be more persuasive. Think of it this way: Why don't you like to change Bibles every five years? That answer is simple: You've learned where certain verses are on certain pages, so your eye naturally looks there. In the same way, you can learn to associate colors with their placement on the page and what they represent. The less attention your notes require, the more persuasive you can be.

present a balanced message. At times, highlighting has helped me to see whether or not my material is balanced. Too much pink and very little blue informs me that I've skimped on Scripture; I have an entertaining speech instead of a sermon. (The colors can also help in editing. If I have two stories that illustrate the same point, and they are in the same color, it may cause me to consider dropping the weaker of the two.)

Why not give this method a try with your next message? Any change from the norm will be confusing at first, but it's well worth the effort and has the potential for a huge payoff in your delivery.

—DS

22 Tapin' It to the Streets

A simple Secret:
Tape your voice; improve your talk.

Want to become a better preacher? Invest a few bucks in a portable tape recorder, and use it to record illustrations and memorize sections of your message. In fact, buying a portable recorder is one of the best investments you'll make in your speaking ministry. Here are some of the benefits:

You can memorize your sermon more easily. If you preach from an outline, you can make your own tape to expedite learning your material. Simply record your talk, and then after you begin to become familiar with it, speak the first line of an illustration or the name of the person you are quoting. Leave blank space on the tape (it worked for Richard Nixon), and then play the tape. When it comes to the blank spots, you fill in the details. Do this several times to reveal the trouble spots and let you know where to place the "prompt lines" on your outline or the cheat sheets in your Bible.

You can practice your sermon more quickly. The tape recorder serves another practical purpose for the preacher. When you're facing crunch time, the final preparation hours prior to preaching can be stressful. It's especially frustrating if you're driving and unable to read your manuscript. I often record the section of my message with which I'm the least familiar. When I listen to that section again and again, the repetition helps me store the section in my short-term memory. Speeding the tape up maximizes my time. I can listen to a ten-minute stretch of my sermon four times in less than half an hour. Amazingly, it stays with me, even at the faster speed.

You can record illustrations before you forget them. You may be thinking, *Why buy a portable recorder when I already have a tape player in my car?* The most basic benefit of a portable tape recorder is that it can record (something your car's tape player can't do).

51

Too often you trust your memory and expect to recall that hilarious joke or insightful statistic you just heard. But when inevitable distractions surface, that precious gem slips from your mind. You are left with the frustration of knowing you had something that would have worked great—and lost it.

If you can record those important details, orally or in writing, then you've got them when you want them. When you hear a joke at lunch or in a speech, simply put the story on tape as you recall it, while it's fresh in your mind. You can also record items straight from your car radio.

Keep two pointers in mind as you go about buying and using a portable tape recorder. First, be sure to select a model with variable speeds; this feature is invaluable. Mine allows me to slow the speed if I'm typing an illustration that I've previously spoken into the recorder. (For those of you who type Christopher Columbus-style—find a key and land on it—you will benefit from putting that baby on the slowest speed possible. Even though your voice will sound like Darth Vader on antihistamines, you'll be able to keep up as you type.)

Second, be sure your portable recorder has a numeric counter. This makes it easier for the person who will be typing the material to locate stories on the tape. Just make certain the counter is on zero when you start to listen to the tape. Then jot down the numbers that appear on the numeric counter each time you come across an illustration you may want to use.

One of the best investments you will ever make is a portable tape recorder. Find one that fits the bill today, buy it, and use it for years to come. Your brain, your typist—and your congregation—will thank you.

—DS

23 And in Conclusion...

A simple Secret:
Your finish booms louder than your start.

People won't necessarily remember how you started, but they will definitely remember a strong finish.

When you say, "And in conclusion," you bring peace and contentment to the flock. The phrase communicates that you've entered the homestretch in this ministerial marathon, the listeners have survived "the wall" and found their second wind, and everyone is now coasting downhill to the finish line. In the midst of your listeners' euphoria, you now have the responsibility of holding their attention, tying all the conceptual loose ends together, and challenging your listeners to some sort of action. The conclusion should put the bow on the package. It should speak loudly and clearly the key biblical truth you want to convey.

Your success here is critical because it is easier to recover from a weak start than a poor finish. So here are some ways you can prepare to finish well:

Memorize your conclusion. Your knowledge of the material will enhance your eye contact and allow you to reach right into listeners' hearts.

Repeat a phrase from earlier in the message to remind people of your theme one last time. This repetition can help "tie the bow" more neatly.

Periodically evaluate your conclusions. Review your last six sermons to see if you're using the same wrap-up method every week. Do you always conclude with a tear-jerker story, a recap of your main points, or some other routine? Vary your methods.

Monitor the body language. As you conclude your message, closely monitor the body language of the people in the pews. What kinds of things are you typically saying that seem to trigger a widespread reach for purses or hymnals? Group fidgeting will teach you volumes about your repetitive habits.

And in conclusion...I don't recommend saying these words because they invite distraction and make your task even tougher.

The simple secret is to invest a higher percentage of your preparation time in your conclusion. Yes, your introduction must capture your listeners' attention, but in the conclusion, you must inspire people to put into practice what they've heard. If you consistently put forth the effort to combine variety with a call to action, then in the end your sermons will be much more effective.

—DS

Reaching Out

Caught in the Act...

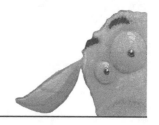

A simple Secret:
Reward your priceless behind-the-scenes heroes.

One of the greatest joys for any pastor is discovering church members who faithfully minister out of the spotlight. They're working for all the right reasons, and the great pastoral secret is: *We can reward these folks*. It doesn't cost a lot of money or time, but it reaps great benefits for the flock, because a word of encouragement from a "professional" to a volunteer is like a nugget of gold.

While preaching a sermon on servanthood several years ago, I mentioned a list of individuals I'd seen using their gifts for God in virtually anonymous ways. One was a man I'd seen vacuuming the hallways outside the sanctuary.

The next week I received a thank-you note from the man. He wrote, "In over forty years of serving the Lord in a variety of ways, I can say that your comment was the first public mention, either in word or in print, of personal acknowledgement for what I try to do. Thank you. It encouraged me."

While I try to write thank-you notes to such behind-the-scenes servants, I recently came up with a more innovative way to recognize those unsung heroes. It's a simple certificate with some money attached to it. On a Saturday afternoon, I may just walk up to a person mowing the lawn, hand him the certificate, and then dash off to my car and drive away. If the particular volunteer is busy in the nursery or helping in the kitchen, I might casually put the certificate in her hands or in her purse while she's hard at work. I like to keep track of the recipients, so if I don't know the individual's name, I may introduce myself and then say, "What is your name?" When he or she tells me, I'll offer the letter and say, "Well, Joe Kemper, this is your special day. You were just caught in the act."

The certificate itself doesn't need to be elaborate. See the next page for an example of what I use, printed on a piece of colored paper.

Certificate of Merit

You have been caught in the act...of serving Jesus Christ. True, there are others who serve in similar ways, but today is your special day!

You may not receive much thanks for the way you serve the Lord and make the church a better fellowship. It's obvious you don't volunteer your time for money or applause. In fact, you are probably rarely appreciated for your out-of-the-spotlight service. Yours is truly a labor of love for the Lord.

What you do may at times seem insignificant. But it isn't. You are letting your light shine so God will be glorified and Southeast Christian Church will be a beacon to others. This is just my way of letting you know you are appreciated.

I noticed your faithfulness, but I want you to know that, more importantly, there is One above who notices too. This small gift is for you in appreciation of your efforts. Please use this money however you would like.

Sincerely,

Dave Stone

Caught in the act of service!

A fellow servant for Christ was caught on

_____,

in this ministry: _____.

"Each one should use whatever gift he has received to serve others,
faithfully administering God's grace in its various forms"
(1 Peter 4:10).

You may place the certificate in an envelope or just fold it twice and clip a $5 or $10 bill to the bottom third of the page. Depending on your preference (and your budget), you may wish to give a certificate once a week or once a month. You might even ask your elders whether the amount could become a budgeted item.

Or just use your own money. When word leaked out about what I'm doing and why, church members came to me and said, "I'd like to help out. Here is some money for the next couple of months."

Remember that your unsolicited and unexpected letter will reward and encourage. It may also breathe new life into a volunteer. In any case, your members will enjoy being caught in the act of serving just as much as you'll enjoy catching them.

—DS

25 Why Aren't You Making Me Grow, Pastor?

A simple Secret:
Spiritual growth is the grower's responsibility.

"*The reason we're no longer attending church is that we weren't growing spiritually.*" I suppose, of all the comments I've heard over the years, this kind has always bothered me most. For a long time, I took such statements personally. Obviously, a particular church won't be the right match for everyone and won't be able to help some individuals grow spiritually. However, more often than not, the folks who complain about a lack of spiritual growth aren't going to grow spiritually regardless of where they worship.

A person's spiritual growth isn't the church's responsibility; it's the individual's. The church can be a resource that assists, guides, and feeds. But the individual Christian needs to take ownership for his or her spiritual growth.

This idea has been quite liberating for me and for our staff. Our goal is to provide all that we can to help people grow. We recognize our responsibility to shepherd, but being sheep is the sheep's job. We can point out green pastures and still waters, but they must choose to eat and drink.

With this perspective, we challenge people in seven areas of spiritual growth and invite them to pursue a balance that will keep them growing. The seven areas are sharing the gospel, personal devotions, financial stewardship, service, relationships, worship, and Bible study. The idea is that we are all on a spiritual journey, needing to grow in our relationship with God, our connection to others, and our impact in the world.

We define the areas of growth because people often feel as if they're growing when they're strong in one particular area. For example, someone may feel very strong in the area of worship but may never use his or her gifts in service. Certainly, a person may have a giftedness and interest that draws him or her deeper in a particular area, but we hope that people will grow in every area. We invite them to do some self-assessment and then create a personal spiritual-development plan.

To help members create a six-month plan that will be relevant to their desires and needs for spiritual growth, our church provides a guide that lists all of the programs, ministries, resources, and options available during the coming six months. Each program or activity is described according to its growth purpose and level of intensity or depth.

Using this guide, people develop a plan that is uniquely theirs, because the church is not a one-size-fits-all enterprise. For example, some people like classes, while others seek hands-on experiences. Some people want video resources and others can use CD-ROMs. This overall approach has put the responsibility for spiritual growth upon the individual and placed the church in the position of providing the means.

I've noticed that people are now creating their own plans for spiritual development and are slowly taking responsibility for what they need to do. A side benefit has been that I rarely hear the comment "I am not growing spiritually at this church."

—RR

What Exactly Are You Building Here?

A simple Secret:
To build a bridge, hop into the stream.

Many people say we should keep our faith to ourselves, out of the workplace, the school, and the public square. Yet it was that great American philosopher Forrest Gump who said, "When you go to the zoo, take some food to feed the animals, even though the signs on the bars say, 'Don't feed the animals.' It wasn't the animals who put those signs up."

People today do want to talk about spiritual issues; they just don't want to talk about them in the same old ways. The most effective way to get a hearing is to build bridges with relationships. And the best way to build relationship bridges is to be in the middle of the stream.

Here's what I mean. The churches that will make a difference in the future will be those that *stand in the stream* and look for ways to disrupt it. That is, they will be intensely involved outside the building's walls. They will minister amid the rough waters where everyday people live their everyday lives apart from Christ.

We certainly must be aware that all the roads leading out of Jerusalem also lead back in. We can't let our efforts to engage the world mold us into becoming the world. But staying within our own walls, just to remain comfortable, says we really don't care. Pulling back and shouting from the banks of the river won't be enough.

If most of the things we're doing are about taking care of us, then we have missed the great heaven-sent challenge of being in the world for others. Therefore, when we look at everything we're doing in our church, we must seriously ask ourselves, *Are we building bridges or building walls? Are we moving outside these walls to disrupt the stream, to make a genuine difference in our communities?* If that's your desire, here are three simple "ins" to help thrust you "out."

Involve yourself on the "outside." Build relationships with those outside of Christ in your community. Get involved in community groups or causes. Encourage your members to volunteer for activities outside the church. Members can effectively use their gifts on Christ's behalf in public schools, sports clubs, and community centers. These and countless other venues offer the chance for believers to rub shoulders with seekers and form lifelong friendships.

Increase your volunteers' influence. Specifically, extend your outreach opportunities by asking local school districts, community agencies, and police departments what you can do to help them. Of course, you can assume they will be suspicious of your motives, but they'll trust you in time if you don't abuse your opportunities for service.

Recently we had a tragedy in our community when a well-known high school student committed suicide. The school called our church and asked if we could send volunteers who would be available to students and staff who wanted to talk. How did that happen? The people who were invited were the same youth coaches who'd been raking pits at track meets, setting up chairs at concerts, and helping to chaperone at dances. Now, in a time of great need, the school staff knew these volunteers could be trusted.

Install "side doors." There's got to be a point of entry in your church for the folks who just won't walk through the front doors. Do you need to knock some doorways into your walls? Consider such outreach "doors" as recovery groups, sports teams, craft groups, grief-support groups, and countless others. Be creative; the list is endless. Focus on anything that genuinely helps people in need while also building relationships.

According to the American Society of Church Growth, half of the churches in America didn't add a single new member through conversion in the year 2000. North America is the only continent where Christianity is not growing, and most so-called church growth can be attributed to people migrating from one congregation to another. It would appear that we have become more adept at building walls than we are at building bridges. How is it on your side of the river?

—RR

27 Go for the Decision

A simple Secret:
Take aim at the people you're targeting.

Sometimes you need a special service in order to have a special emphasis, in order to reach special people for purposes that are, well...*special.* For example, we offer a particular service each year that makes all the difference to our growth and ongoing enthusiasm for outreach. We call it Decision Day, the special Sunday morning when we encourage people who haven't done so to make this the day they make a decision to accept Christ or become a member. The target group is people who've been attending for a year or more, and we've discovered that the large-group format of Decision Day lessens the anxiety of those who have been hesitating to make a decision.

Decision Day is just one example of a special service, and you will no doubt come up with several of your own. But here's a brief overview of what we do to make Decision Day a great day in our church.

• To set the stage throughout the year, we staff a Decision Room each weekend and invite people who have questions about their relationship with God or questions about our church. People who just need to talk or pray come there too. Staffing the room has become a regular part of our ministry.

• We determine the date for Decision Day six months in advance. Then we schedule classes and seminars geared toward assisting people in coming to Christ. Leading up to Decision Day, sermons and lessons focus on making a commitment to Christ and his church.

• Eight weeks before the scheduled day, we meet with counselors, elders, staff, and the prayer team to pray for our targeted individuals.

• Five weeks out, we send letters to people to invite them to the classes and seminars and tell them about Decision Day.

• Four weeks in advance, we call all those on our list to invite them to Decision Day and ask if there is anything we can help with or if they have questions.

• Three weeks out, we send a letter from the senior minister, asking if there is any way the church can assist them in this important decision.

• Two weeks prior to this special Sunday, we continue the phone calls, follow-up meetings, and training sessions with decision counselors.

• After Decision Day, we use all of our normal follow-up methods for new Christians and new members. In addition, we seek to meet any unique personal needs or requests coming from our new members.

This special service has become one of the few days when we invite people to come forward in our church services. We've been doing this for six years and have never had fewer than a hundred people respond. Our advance work seems to prepare the ground for a fertile harvest. It has been a blessing to our church and is viewed in a very positive light. This annual event allows us to reach out to people who have been attending for quite a while but have yet to make a decision.

—RR

28 Make It Special

A simple Secret:
Special-interest events will reach special new people.

In Matthew 13, Jesus tells of a farmer scattering seed. Some seeds grew and brought about a harvest, while other seeds didn't. What could happen if you planned some church services with the intent of scattering seed on brand-new soil? Special services throughout the year draw visitors into your ministry circle where they can be reached with the gospel message. Here are a few special events that have worked effectively for us as we sought to sow good seed:

Friends Day. Encourage everyone to bring a guest on this day. This event serves a twofold purpose. First, it motivates your members to invite people, if they aren't already in the habit of doing that. Second, it's easier for friends to accept the invitation because they know they won't be the *only* guests.

If you face sanctuary-space limitations or parking challenges, you may decide to have a Friends Month. The added time spreads out the increased attendance. It also removes the "I can't come that Sunday because I have to shampoo my hair" kind of excuses because you can respond, "Well, how about coming with us the next week?"

Victory Day. This idea originated with Max Lucado at his church in San Antonio, Texas. He publicly recognizes those who made a commitment to Christ in the previous year. A good time for a Victory Day service is the end of December or beginning of January. To get a higher level of participation, send a letter informing the new members of the service a couple of weeks before it's scheduled.

Here's how it works. During a regular worship service, read the names of those who made a decision for Christ during the past year and invite them to join you at the front of the church. (You may also seat them in the choir loft or have them stand on risers.) Honor and encourage those who made decisions for Christ. You might even ask them to say a word or two about how things are going for them and if they would like to voice a prayer request. This gives everyone an opportunity to celebrate the harvest of the entire year.

Dedication Day. This service is for the new babies in your congregation. Just as Hannah presented Samuel before the Lord, parents are given the opportunity to dedicate their children to him. Several times a year we reserve part of our service for this purpose. Here's one approach:

• To promote the event the preceding Sunday, project baby pictures on a screen during your announcements.

• When it's time to present the babies to the church, lead parents with their babies to the front during a congregational song.

• Announce the name of each baby and parent as the nursery director hands parents a certificate and a Bible.

• Before the dedication prayer, ask that extended family members stand and be identified with each child. In this way you will welcome relatives who have never been to your church—because they love that baby.

• After the service, people seated nearby can welcome the babies, parents, and relatives.

When planning any special events, make certain you are prepared with ample materials to acquaint visitors with your church and to inform them of upcoming events and opportunities.

A word of caution, though, when it comes to annual special events: Sometimes it's healthy to take a break for a year or two rather than watch a good program gradually die a slow death. What worked well during the past ten years may not be effective during the next five. Your purpose, after all, is to come up with different creative emphases that will attract people to your church and give them a positive memory of the experience. When the Spirit of the Lord blesses that service, your visitors may just return.

—DS

The Wedding Planner

A simple Secret:
Tying the marriage knot requires planning and practice.

At any given wedding, a candle may not light...or it may fall over. The groom may sweat. The bride may cry. A groomsman may faint. The ring may be forgotten, and the father of the bride might not be speaking to his first wife and her new boyfriend. Since women often marry men who are like their fathers, the mother of the bride usually cries through it all!

Early in my ministry I heard a friend say that he would much rather preach a funeral than a wedding. When I asked why, he simply responded, "Less pressure. At a funeral there are fewer opportunities for things to go wrong, and there is one less person to complain."

How true! Still, while many things are out of your control at a wedding, you *can* improve the chances that the service will go smoothly. Two things, in particular, require concentrated attention: your final premarital appointment with the couple and the dress rehearsal.

The important final appointment comes at the end of premarital classes or counseling. At this meeting, be sure to

• go over the order of the service.

• ask about any Scriptures the couple wants to include.

• identify any departed family members the couple wants to honor, as well as any subjects to avoid.

• ask each person, "Why did you choose this individual to become your spouse? Describe him/her for me." Then write down exactly what each person says.

• if you don't already know how the couple met and how they became engaged, ask them. Write their responses on a note card, and place it with your notes for the service. Sharing how these two met, and what they appreciate about each other, makes the service personal and more meaningful to all.

• focus on God's Word and the couple's lifelong commitment and tie the knot tightly! If you ask the right questions and take good notes in that final meeting, then 90 percent of your work for the wedding is done.

At the wedding rehearsal, everything will run more smoothly if you keep these four guidelines in mind:

1. Utilize your church's wedding coordinator. This allows the pastor to say yes to more weddings and still have Friday nights free. Explain this to the bride when the wedding is scheduled. If you are close with the family, you may choose to join the wedding party at the rehearsal dinner.

2. Identify who is in charge of the rehearsal. There can be only one chief that the people will follow.

3. Give special attention to locations. Be clear and certain about where everyone will stand, the directions they will face, the cues for them to move, and the time to arrive for pictures the next day. Begin by having all the participants stand in the positions they will be in after the father and the bride have just walked down the aisle. Slowly walk through the wedding service and practice exiting. Then start at the beginning with the processional and quickly go through the service again, ending with the recessional.

4. Study the names of the couple. Their names should roll off of your tongue with ease. Avoid the embarrassment of having to look down at your notes for pronunciation cues!

Even if you don't know the couple well, the service will likely proceed smoothly if you are prepared. And while weddings may be more stressful than funerals, you can still provide comfort, encouragement, and spiritual guidance on a very special day. Most important, you can help a starry-eyed new couple start down the pathway to a godly marriage.

—DS

Timesaving and Efficiency

How to
Read a Book

A simple Secret:
Useful reading trumps voluminous reading.

If you teach at a university, you aren't worth your salt if you don't produce a book. The mantra is *publish or die.* In ministry, though, it's *read or die.*

That's why, nearly twenty years ago, I made a commitment to read. And I kept a single-minded focus, not on the volume of material, but on what I was getting out of it. Actually reading a book is only half the point. For years I would read and then forget what I had found so relevant and inspiring. I was missing out on *making reading useful.* Sadly, I was forgoing the creation of a deep well of useful material that I could draw upon, as needed, down the road.

Not that I lacked the desire to remember it all. Even in my early years, I'd underline and highlight my way through just about every book. The highlighting and underlining aided my recall but still left me dependent on my memory. Later—perhaps years later—I'd think, *Seems like there's something about that in x-y-z book.* Then I'd spend valuable time thumbing through that book and skimming all those yellow, pink, and blue paragraphs.

Any of us can implement a better method and increase our capacity for making reading useful. For me, a better method required two simple steps. First, when I find something useful, I write the beginning of the sentence and the page number in the back of the book. If necessary, I summarize the main idea of the passage. This allows me to grab a book and very quickly, by scanning the back few pages, find the source, quote, or idea that I need.

Second, as I'm reading the book, I mark the margins with my own set of hieroglyphics. Later, my administrative assistant, who is well-versed in hieroglyphics translation, types, scans, or photocopies and files everything by topic. In this way, material I've read last week—or years ago—is instantly retrievable. This week, as I'm preparing a lesson or message on marriage, for instance, I can type in the topic and immediately peruse quotes, illustrations, ideas, or even books on the topic. It's a bit like subscribing to one of those quotation services, but it's better because it's not "generic" stuff; it all flows from my own personal reading program. The material has already made an impact on my soul, so I can preach it with genuine passion.

Read or die. Read usefully, no matter how many books you can get through in a month. Read to fill the well that so often runs low. Read to keep yourself fresh and current. (Read because, after all, somebody has published a book, and if you don't read it, how will the writer eat?)

—RR

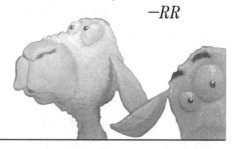

31 Doing... but Why?

A simple Secret:
The biggest hindrance to achievement is unharnessed activity.

It's said that a former president of Avis corporation put a sign on his desk, over his office doorway, in his car, and on his bathroom mirror. It asked, "Is what I am now doing, or about to do, going to make Avis number one?"

I'm not too concerned about whether Avis is number one. But as we look at our busy days, our busy weeks, and our busy lives, we might ask ourselves, *Is what I am now doing, or about to do, going to help me accomplish the primary goal of my life?*

Typically, when we attempt to answer such a question, we begin by making a list of all the things we're doing and then decide to say no to some of them. I have discovered that I say no quite well; however, it's learning to say yes better that can make the big difference. In other words, we often begin at the wrong end of the problem by creating our lists of activities and determining which we can no longer attend. Let's begin at the other end of the stick by looking at the big three achievement components: purposes, goals, and activities.

First let's ask ourselves (and our organizations) exactly what we want to be. That is, what are our ultimate purposes? Responses might range from "I want to be a stronger leader" or "I want to be a more effective communicator" to "I want to be a better father." These "to be" statements are direction setters. By themselves they are difficult to measure or define. For example, what does "I want to be a better father" mean? If this is what we want to be, how will we know after six weeks if we have become better fathers? Yet this is the first step in beginning to control our time. It's setting direction and deciding what we want to be.

Our second step is to give clarity and relevance to our purpose statements by setting specific goals. For example, if one of my purposes is "to be a better father," then what things will I plan to do in order to *become* a better father?

As you probably know, good goals have a definite beginning, a definite ending, and checkpoints along the way. They are brutally specific, not fuzzy. "I want to be a better father" could have several goals attached to it. Here are some possibilities.

Goal: "Beginning December 10, I will spend Monday evenings with my children doing something they like to do. I will do this for three months and then evaluate the effects."

Goal: "Starting next Tuesday, I will have lunch with one of my children so that every three weeks I'm meeting with each of my kids individually over lunch. I will do this throughout the fall school term."

After four Mondays or four Tuesdays have passed, will I be a better father? I don't know for sure. But I can know whether I did indeed spend the time with my children that I said I would.

The third step, after developing *purposes* and *goals*, relates to our level of *activity*. What are we are actually doing? Are the things we're doing the things we said we wanted to do, in order to become what we wanted to become? If not, then why are we doing them?

It works best if purpose sits in judgment of goals and goals sit in judgment of activity. Thus we keep asking,

What do we want to be?

What will we do to become *that?*

What are we actually doing?

If we continue to ask these questions, we will find that the single biggest hindrance to achieving our purposes is often the proliferation of activity. We are doing too much. On the other hand, if we start at the right end of the problem, by discerning our true purposes and creating the practical goals to accomplish them, we can—with less guilt and more confidence—say yes to that which helps us achieve our highest potential.

—RR

Pull the Plug on Distraction

A simple Secret:
Focus—and feel the power surge.

Several years ago I heard leadership guru Jim Collins tell about his goal of reading a hundred books a year. The first night he sat down with a book in his hand, he also began watching *Monday Night Football.* The game was more exciting than the book, so Collins watched football. Soon he realized that in order to read his hundred books, he'd have to unplug his television. Collins looked at the group of Christian leaders and asked the million-dollar question, "What must *you* unplug in order to accomplish your goals?"

When you arrive at your own individual answer, you must adjust your schedule accordingly, regardless of the pain, in order to enjoy a newfound ability to focus. Here's how to begin:

Hop off the "pleaser plane." Our hearts can soar into the clouds when it appears we've made someone happy. We ministers love to please people and help them in every way. But pleasing people is not our primary objective. "Approved unto God" is supposed to rate higher on the Christian's list of priorities. So while the church or organization experiences growth and new challenges, the pastor or leader must become more and more protective of his or her schedule.

Consider study essential. You might be a great preacher, but if you can't carve out the time to fully research, study, and prepare your sermons, your messages will stagnate over time. Excellence will be forced out in order to make room for the status quo. Jean de la Bruyere, a French writer of the 1600s, put it this way: "There are certain things in which mediocrity is intolerable: poetry, music, painting, public eloquence. What torture it is to hear a frigid speech being pompously declaimed, or second-rate verse spoken with all a bad poet's bombast!" Don't let that be the case when it comes to your work in the pulpit. Study hard; avoid mediocrity.

Do a yes-and-no inventory. Once you've thoroughly surveyed your time-use tendencies, determine to say no to the many optional responsibilities and yes to the crucial few. Failure to do so will result in stagnation, mediocrity, and goals that can't be accomplished. It won't be easy, because ministers face the same major barrier that other leaders do: There aren't enough hours in the day. Thus it's easy to be stretched thin and pulled in many directions.

If your congregation is growing, the solution is to remove less important responsibilities as new, more important ones are added to your plate. In fact, there's a basic leadership principle here that deserves the attention of every pastor: *Only do what only you can do.* It may not sound profound, but living by this basic principle will profoundly increase your effectiveness.

The bottom line is to keep asking yourself the right questions:

Are there any volunteers who could shoulder some of my increasing responsibilities?

How could I be freed to minister more efficiently and effectively in this changing situation?

Where does my ministry derive the greatest benefit from my time?

Have the courage to focus on truly reaching your potential for Christ. Pull the plug on a few energy-draining distractions, and you'll experience the power surge that focus can bring to your ministry.

—DS

Unannounced, but Not Unwelcome

A simple Secret:
You can prevent disruptions from disrupting you.

A number of years ago, a new and relatively young staff person stopped by my office to ask me how to handle people who just drop by his office. As I got up from my chair and walked toward him, I said that I would love to show him how to politely assist people who just drop in. As we headed toward my door, I asked him how often it was happening. As we continued toward the hallway, I suggested that we could schedule a time soon to talk about it. As we arrived in the hallway, I told him that we could figure out how best to do this without being rude.

Later, I called him and asked him if he knew now how to politely handle someone who dropped by his office. He said, "No, not at all." Then I asked him where he was and where I was. Only then did he realize he no longer needed to schedule time to talk about the issue.

Rarely do people who "just drop by" have a pressing, legitimate need. One of the difficulties of ministry is knowing when and how to handle these disruptions without appearing to be out of reach or uncaring. Here are some of my own methods:

At the office—It used to be that when a person came to my office unannounced, I would have my assistant assess the need and either handle the request or schedule an appointment. It kept me out of the loop but began to seem a little too "corporate" for me. So I've returned to taking a minute or two to speak with the individual personally. The one or two minutes I take with a person will often save me the ten minutes I'd spend wondering whether a visitor really did have a legitimate need. And often two minutes is all the person really needed or wanted in the first place. It's easy to ask what is on the person's mind and quickly assess if the issue needs immediate attention. (But I always make sure the one- or two-minute meeting does not take place in my office.)

Of course, another person may need to help some of these folks; they may need to talk to a youth coach, a teacher, or a board member, for instance. However, if they really do need to see me, I ask them to schedule an appointment before introducing them to my calendar keeper. (If you are the keeper of your own calendar, suggest a time: "How about next Tuesday at 2:00?" This communicates your genuine interest, while allowing you to return to what you were working on.)

On the phone—With the aid of voice mail or an answering machine, we have no need to enslave ourselves to ringing phones. Just leave a recorded message that gives people an opportunity to let you know what they need. Then schedule a regular time to listen to messages and return phone calls at your convenience.

Do return your own phone calls, though. I hate receiving calls only to be asked by a secretary to hold while so-and-so gets on the line (unless, of course, so-and-so is the president).

In the home—Again, who said that every time the phone rings we need to drop all we're doing and jump to answer it? (Have you ever received a call late at night or early in the morning, and the caller says, "I hope you weren't sleeping"? Weren't you tempted to respond, "No, no, I was just sitting here waiting for my phone to ring"?) Here's where you just let the answering machine screen your calls for you. Spend the $8 a month on caller ID. It can genuinely improve the quality of your family time. Since we instituted a rule about not answering the phone during mealtimes, our quality time together has begun to stretch from the moment we enter the house in the evening until we leave again the next day.

People do matter, and we certainly want to be attentive to people and their needs. But don't forget the renowned management principle: "The urgent is seldom important, and the important is seldom urgent."

—RR

Prepare to Be Great

A simple Secret:
With a pre-game routine, your sermons won't be routine.

I was fortunate to play college basketball. (OK, so it might be a stretch to say I played, but I did have a great seat on the bench.) Before every game we followed this set routine: a curfew the night before to ensure proper rest, a walk-through five hours before game time, a pre-game meal (including steak) three hours before the game. An hour before the game, we stretched, shot around, and warmed up. Finally, just before game time, we received a strategy speech from our coach followed by the Lord's Prayer.

Why do the same thing before every game? There's a simple explanation for this discipline: The routine bolsters your confidence as you successfully complete each step.

It only stands to reason that preachers could benefit from a standard sermon-preparation routine. It's helpful to know whether you are truly prepared or behind schedule. When you get into a good rhythm, your message preparation can flow if you stay true to your strategy.

Ministers' preparation styles and time constraints differ, and each of us has experienced those crunch times when an unexpected funeral or the surgery waiting room subtracts hours you had originally allocated to sermon preparation. Of course, the Lord usually helps with inspiration if you've been diligent with the time you *did* have. But do develop your own, personalized timeline, and try to make it a matter of routine. Here is a sample of how I approach my sermon prep "pre-game" timeline:

Months in advance: Ongoing prayer that God will give me a relevant, life-changing message for those who will hear it.

Weeks in advance: Select series, sermon titles, and main texts.

Monday: Read related material and illustrations on the topic.

Wednesday: Brainstorm possible outlines and lines of thinking.

Thursday afternoon: Finalize outline and continue writing.

Friday afternoon: Have thirteen or fourteen pages of material gathered.

Saturday, 1 p.m.: Have material edited to about ten pages.

Saturday afternoon: E-mail manuscript to tech crew and interpreters for the deaf.

Saturday early evening: Read aloud, and highlight with markers.

Saturday late evening: Preach the Word in Saturday night worship.

Saturday late night: Make adjustments for Sunday according to voice mail suggestions.

Sunday morning: Preach the revised version in Sunday services.

Don't get too attached to my example. It's simply a method that works for me in my particular situation. You need to determine what works best for you—but I can virtually guarantee that if you develop a regular preparation routine you'll be anything but routine with your results.

—DS

35 Great Things Happen When You Plan

A simple Secret:
You can plan a sermon road map for the spiritual journey of your church.

More and more churches are trying to plan their worship services well in advance. This planning allows them to weave a common theme throughout the music, drama, and preaching. For the common theme to be used successfully, sermon topics must be chosen early in the process so that each component of worship can build on the others. In addition, this kind of planning allows pastors to plan where they want to lead their churches on the spiritual journey in the months and years ahead.

Not only will you breathe easier knowing *where* you want to lead your people in the Word, you'll also feel more confident about *how* you're all going to get there. I've found that the benefits of planning ahead take care of the big challenges of preaching:

Planning ahead removes the "topic block." You've heard of writer's block? Preachers can suffer a similar kind of paralysis each Monday morning as they consider what topic to preach at the next service. For me, half the battle is determining the topic or text. Once I know the topic, I can create file folders and documents on my computer to gather the relevant material I come across weeks in advance. This material primes the pump and helps me overcome the fear of not knowing what to say next week.

Planning ahead gives you the big picture. What areas have you already covered in your ministry? Which topics and themes have you mostly neglected? Your sermon road map will help you continue to answer such questions through the years. Our preaching and worship team knows that we need to devote some pulpit time every two years to stewardship, evangelism, marriage and family, Bible study, service, and so on.

Planning frees you to make changes. Planning takes the monkey off the preacher's back as Sunday morning approaches. If necessary, you always have the freedom to make changes or to completely scrap a series—well in advance—and put together one that will be more relevant to a new situation.

If you've never tried planning your sermon series further forward than just a week or two, consider following these simple guidelines:

Schedule a planning meeting. Every October we bring together several of our staff members, along with any other preachers in the area, who might be preaching. We block out most of a day for this planning meeting and we chart out the coming year.

Brainstorm ahead. The week before the planning meeting, I usually peruse listings of sermon series in the tape catalogs published by prominent ministries. These catalogs simulate creativity and bring to mind topics that we may not have covered in recent years.

Come prepared. We ask each person to bring to the meeting a number of different series ideas, complete with possible titles and texts. Each person should have enough copies of each series to distribute to the others.

Pitch and tweak ideas. We ask each person to pitch one series idea. The group then offers suggestions on how to tweak the series in order to make it more effective.

Check the calendar. We keep a copy of the next year's calendar available for constant reference. We also have a copy of the past three years' preaching calendars to remind us of what has already been covered. (Note: Placement is key. For example, Easter is a great time to complete a series on Jesus and to promote a new series on a hot topic starting the next weekend. The guest whose curiosity is piqued may return and, over time, make a commitment to the Lord.)

Vote for favorites. We then vote on the top themes and series that resonate most deeply with the group. We begin to place these in the calendar with specific topics and specific dates. (Note: Our goal is not to complete all of our planning at that particular meeting. The following week, we block out an hour to place finishing touches on the plan or to modify a series that may have generated second thoughts.)

Planning need not be a noose around your neck. View it instead as a road map for the spiritual growth of your church. The amount of time you take isn't as important as the actual discipline of planning. It will give you great peace of mind to know that you're mapping out a journey that you and your flock will all enjoy together.

—DS

Church Management

Calling All Eagles (and Pigeons)

A simple Secret:
It's smarter to work smart.

You know the type—the eagles. They soar above the rest of us in all the right categories: productivity, accomplishment, success. They're the naturally athletic, the musical, the handy, the oh-so-organized, the perfectly analytical. With so little effort, they make things happen, using their gifts with such ease that everything seems effortless.

We're the pigeons. If we obtain good results, it comes with great effort. Whether we're pigeons or eagles, though, Scripture tells us that God has gifted each of us (see 1 Peter 4:10) and that our gifts were meant to be used. As French novelist Emile Zola once said, "The artist is nothing without the gift, but the gift is nothing without work."

And God does expect us to work. Amazingly, he has chosen us to be his hands and his feet here on earth. We are to give voice to his story and flesh to his love. Eagles and pigeons alike have been given the gifts to carry out this work. The problem is that we are often ineffective. We get bogged down and overwhelmed. We rush around putting out brush fires and seldom get to the real issues. So we live in this trap of having gifts and under-utilizing them because we work so poorly.

How can you work more effectively? Assuming you know your gifts and are working in a ministry that fits, you can benefit from a few simple suggestions for doing eagle-like work, even if you're one of the pigeons:

1. Plan. What is the work to be done, and how do you go about doing it? Create a plan for the work you are doing. Get help if you don't know how; some people have this gift.

2. Begin. The hardest part of any task is getting started. A typical shuttle mission will use millions of pounds of fuel as the spacecraft travels thousands of miles. However, most of the fuel is burned up in the launch.

Similarly, the start-up phase of your project will use up lots of your energy; nevertheless, go ahead and begin. As one Army general put it, "A good plan executed now is better than the best plan executed later."

3. Focus. Unless you're Superman, you can only do so many things at once. Therefore, prioritize. Which efforts will bring the greatest return? A corollary of Pareto's Principle says that 20 percent of our effort will produce 80 percent of the results, while 80 percent of our effort only produces 20 percent of the results. What are the "20 percent things" you can do today?

4. Serve. When our work is viewed as serving, it doesn't seem so much like work. As someone once said, "Life is like a game of tennis; the player who serves well seldom loses."

5. Finish. When asked what made for a successful life, Henry Ford is said to have replied, "Always finish what you start." Keep a to-do list if you have to, build in accountability, and do whatever it takes to see each task to the end.

Zola was right that the gift is nothing without the work. But to get the work done, we must work smart and effectively. Eagles and pigeons alike only get to hear the words *well done* when we well do.

$$-RR$$

37 Who's in Charge of Your Time?

A simple Secret:
Those "mail things" can become your friends.

You pick up your phone and discover fourteen new messages and eight old ones. You open your e-mail and find thirty-six people wanting something. At first these "mail things" are wonderful conveniences; then you begin hating the little blinking light and that irritating "You've got mail!" cyber-guy. (Someone has said that having e-mail "is like coming home after a long day and finding a dozen people standing in your kitchen.") Yet these tools can be a huge help to our ministries—they can even be our friends—as long as they don't overwhelm us.

You've already discovered that you don't actually *have* to talk to anyone. You can let a person's voice mail leave your voice mail a message. (You know the trick: If someone's been bugging you to respond, you find out when he or she goes to lunch, return the call at that time, and leave a message similar to this: "Sorry I missed you, but I'm departing on a missions trip and will look forward to catching up with you when I return in three years. Have a good day.")

I have a colleague whose voice mail greeting is "Hi. You have reached John. I promise I'll listen to your message." I like that. No promise of a return call. No promise he'll do anything other than listen to my message.

In other words, if we use them wisely, voice mail and e-mail can be useful tools in managing our days. The key is simply deciding who's in charge—you or the message. Once you decide you're going to be the boss, consider these tips:

Schedule. Pick certain times of the day, several probably, when you will check your "mails." Don't drop what you're doing just because some little light is flashing.

Respond. When you do check your various mails, respond in some fashion *immediately.* If you're reading e-mail, delete, reply, or forward. In some cases, file a message for later response; make a list of the things you've been requested to do and attach due dates. When you check phone messages, either return the call or forward the messages to appropriate people within your church.

Delete. Do use that delete key liberally. It's a wonderful little device when you see a forwarded message. If the forwarded message happens to be useful (how rare!), a quick thanks is the only response needed.

Conserve. Save time and energy by doing as much as you can electronically. Many meeting notices and quick responses can be accomplished through e-mail. Send agendas, ideas, and files through cyberspace. Save people the time of physically meeting about trivial issues; just ask them to respond to your message. And remember, using master lists of e-mail groups allows you to easily and quickly keep in touch with all of the people who need the same message.

Long ago I was told that the most effective way to deal with my mail (snail mail) was to handle the paper only one time—answer it, pass it on, file it, or throw it away. Making any other choice just meant I was building up piles of future work. While technology has added different kinds of "mails" to our lives, we still ought to handle each piece only once.

The bottom line is that we need to control our mail and not let it control us. Almost everyone I know who feels plowed under by mail hasn't learned to respond in some fashion right away. Pretty soon stuff accumulates, and the recipient becomes overwhelmed by "mail things" that begin to look like the enemy.

—RR

Underwhelmed Secretary?

A simple Secret:
Get more assistance from your assistant.

Recently I held a seminar for people whose primary responsibility is assisting their bosses. The number one complaint I heard from them was that they felt underutilized. If you're fortunate enough to have an assistant, secretary, personal valet—or whatever you choose to call the person who will eventually do all your thinking—you are blessed. But is this person benefiting you to the fullest? Consider these do's and don'ts as you attempt to help your assistant become of greater assistance:

Do **pay attention to the vibes.** Your assistant will often be the first impression *you* make. Be sure it's the impression you want. This isn't a matter of physical appearance as much as attitude. Is the person under consideration naturally open and gracious with others? willing to listen and respond with good will? inviting and encouraging to visitors, church members, and staff alike, whether in person or over the phone? generally optimistic, conveying a can-do spirit, and not prone to gossip?

Answering such questions *before* hiring an assistant could be critical to your own future success.

Do **communicate, communicate, communicate!** Clearly define your expectations, and set up regular performance reviews. Remember that it takes time for a person to learn how you prefer doing things. Be patient, and keep talking about what you need. Work hard not to make poor planning on your part into a crisis for your assistant. I've watched assistants suffer the consequences of a project's sloppiness or lateness when it was clearly not their fault. It's just that the plan wasn't clearly communicated up front. When you perceive a potential problem with a project, be direct about confronting it immediately.

Do **build the level of trust.** Give your assistant enough information and authority to complete a project or handle an ongoing responsibility. If you hope your assistant will begin responding to things the way you would, allow him or her to know how you arrive at certain conclusions and how you like things to be approached. Discuss who gets priority, what projects matter most to you, which things you want to know about, and which you do not. In other words, invite assistants into the process. You'll improve their effectiveness—and improve your own effectiveness sooner—if you give them insight into your style.

Don't *assume* **everything's going smoothly.** You'd like to think everything is proceeding according to your plan. But have you checked into things lately? If changes are needed, it's better to know sooner rather than later. As assistants learn your style, you will also learn theirs. You will know which things to follow up on and which to trust are being done. A good manager needs to be a little lazy and a little mean. You need to be willing to give away some work and then hold people accountable. Ultimately, an effective assistant has the ability to respond to many of the matters that used to consume much of your time. You'll have no involvement, or very minimal review involvement, in some things. And that's a good thing!

Don't keep your schedule a secret. As soon as possible, let your assistant control your calendar. Give him or her the opportunity to keep you on track and make sure you're where you're supposed to be when you're supposed to be there. (Calendar tip: Keep only one calendar.) Meet with your assistant early each week or at the beginning of each day. This will allow you to review the day and week, set priorities, and review current projects. This is a great time for fielding questions and offering clarifications.

Don't forget respect. Always treat your assistant with the utmost courtesy and the highest regard. An assistant who is respected will usually speak highly of you, even when you're out of earshot, and work just as hard when you're out of the office. Always remember that respect is a two-way street. I continue to be amazed by the number of "bosses" who treat their assistants as if they were simply hired help. In the consulting work I do, I've discovered that the best bosses have often been the best subordinates. They remember what it was like.

Sometimes we think we can cut corners and do just a little less than the best; after all, this is merely for the church. But is it right to do shoddy work for the Lord? Therefore, never underestimate the power of letting capable people take tasks from you. This approach values others and frees you. If your assistants are good at what they do, they make *you* better.

—RR

How Flexible?

A simple Secret:
Not everyone will like the changes.

How often have we clung to methods simply because "we've always done it that way before"? I know of a church that kept a white tablecloth over the elements of the Lord's Supper. Each week before the Lord's Supper was served, the cloth was removed and folded before the elements were distributed. It was a ritual; it was part of their custom in serving the Lord's Supper. Then a new minister came to the church and asked, *"Why?"*

No one knew.

He continued his search until he discovered a lady in her nineties who had the answer. She said that for years the church wasn't air-conditioned. When the windows were opened in the summer, the flies got into the grape juice, so they covered up the elements. Now, with an air-conditioned sanctuary, the ritual could change.

Change isn't easy, of course, but it is often necessary. We live in a day and age of rapid change, yet we often remain unchanged in our approaches to ministry. At seminars I often ask, "How many of you have a cell phone? How many have a DVD player or new VCR? How many have microwave ovens? How many have a computer, laptop, Palm Pilot? How many of you drive a vehicle newer than a 1996 model?"

Nearly every hand in the room will be raised several times. Then I ask, "Why is it that we are not content to operate in our homes, businesses, and personal lives without utilizing the conveniences and technology that can make us operate better, but we are driving models of ministry on 2002 highways with methods from the '90s, '60s, or even '50s?"

I am absolutely convinced that we have a responsibility to take the gospel that never changes to a world that will never be the same. In other words, the message of hope and grace through Christ is the same yesterday, today, and forever, but the methods by which that message is delivered, communicated, and distributed must change with the times. So how can we—with the least amount of pain—introduce change to our congregations?

The simple secret is this: *Don't assume that everyone will like the idea.* Expect the critics, and plan how you'll respond to the questions and challenges that will come.

Because I knew there would be a significant need for change when I arrived at this congregation, I invited a group of former leaders and older members to a once-a-month meeting. This group has been affectionately called the Gray-Hair Group. I told these folks that I needed to hear their advice and seek their wisdom. I wanted this time to share with them what the new leadership team was doing and why. There were three rules: (1) I would tell them everything I knew about what the church was doing, (2) any reaction or opinion was fine to share, and (3) there would be no voting.

It has been ten years, and the group still meets, open to anyone who would like to attend. Over the years this group has often given me valuable advice, particularly about how to frame the things I'll be communicating to the rest of the congregation. And the group has often been the most supportive when change was being implemented.

Of course, not every change will work, no matter how many meetings we have. In every enterprise there is a dynamic tension between maintenance and development; this is no less true in the church. Effective leaders know their job is to manage the tension. They do it by communicating *why* they are seeking change, making sure that people have plenty of input, and not tackling the entire elephant unless there is broad support. They establish some small wins before implementing more difficult or substantive changes. Trust develops, and the plans can usually proceed.

Change isn't easy, and it isn't easy for people to change. But the church is, has been, and always will be about change. The key is to keep creating and re-creating the environment that is most fruitful for the growth of God's kingdom.

—RR

Beware the Business Blunders

A simple Secret:
Mistakes that kill businesses can kill churches, too.

People have different standards for measuring success. A little boy asked his grandpa, "Can you make a sound like a frog?"

"Yes, but why do you ask?"

"Because," the little boy responded, "Mom said when you croak we'll be rich."

Money, power, numbers, influence—people and organizations use these measures to determine their success or effectiveness. In ministry it can be more difficult to measure whether we're succeeding or failing.

But while we're asking whether we're successful, we could inquire of ourselves, *Have we avoided deadly mistakes?* It's a good question to ask, because we'll certainly know we're *not* successful if we've killed our ministries!

Years ago one of the tools we began to use in our church was a normal business-planning tool, similar to the one you're probably already using. We asked each staff member to write a plan, with goals and objectives, for each of his or her ministries. We were expecting to be productive with certain businesslike approaches. But we also knew that businesses sometimes make mistakes that can cause them to fail. And we wanted to keep them in mind—those common, though deadly, business blunders.

Not knowing the customer. For the church, not knowing the customer translates into not knowing who we are serving or trying to reach.

Failing to plan for the future. Simply put, failure to plan is not having a clear vision of what God would have us do and having no specific strategy to accomplish our mission.

Underutilizing technology. This underutilization may include the pastor who can't use a computer and doesn't have voice mail. In myriad ways, not taking advantage of technology can send the message that people must tailor their needs to our ability to meet them.

Ignoring employees. Churches may make poor use of volunteers, neglecting to give them responsibility and the authority to carry out their ministries.

Running out of money. Churches that fail to teach stewardship can find themselves in a financial crisis. We must be sure that everything we have—our time, talent, treasure, opportunity, and influence—is being used for purposes that advance the kingdom.

Ignoring bottom-line issues. This means failing to pay attention to the things that *can* be measured in the church. By trying to do everything, instead of doing only the things we do well, we allow our focus to drift.

Doing it all on their own. There are church leaders—amazingly enough—who forget to include God in the process. Remember: "In his heart a man plans his course, but the Lord determines his steps" (Proverbs 16:9).

I have friends who sit around waiting for God to zap them with a vision for ministry. I have other friends who make their own plans and never consult God. I am convinced that God has gifted each of us with the ability to think, dream, plan, counsel, and strategize. When we remain open to his leading, when we bathe the process in prayer, it is God who provides direction and keeps us from ultimate failure. So we ask our ministry teams to make plans, but we also ask them to avoid the deadly mistakes that lurk in the shadows in any organization pursuing success.

—RR

Leadership

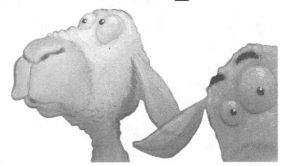

41 The Designer Is...*Here*

A simple Secret:
Effective leaders protect their quiet times.

While I was writing this book, I spoke at a church in Fort Worth, Texas. Being a gracious host, the preacher, Rick, took me to play golf at the Preston Trail Golf Club. It's a prestigious course, quite difficult to get onto, designed in 1963 by a man who was better known as a golfer than a designer. In fact, he was probably the greatest golfer ever to play the game: Byron Nelson. To put it in perspective, in 2000 Tiger Woods enjoyed the hottest streak in professional golf in over fifty years by winning five consecutive tournaments. Quite impressive, until you realize that in 1945 Byron Nelson won eleven straight tournaments. He dominated the sport.

Rich in history because of Nelson, Preston Trail is also gorgeous, immaculate, first-class in every way. And the course (like most) brought me to my knees. But playing that course wasn't the highlight of my day.

If you are a golfer you may be wondering, *What could have been more special, on that day, than playing Preston Trail?* Well, it occurred later that evening. After preaching, I had shaken a number of hands, visited with several people, and was getting ready to head out, when an elderly man approached me. I recognized him.

He said, "Great sermon. I enjoyed it."

"Thank you," I said. "And I enjoyed playing your golf course today, Mr. Nelson."

Then I kind of stuttered, "I'm...I'm honored to meet you." Here was Byron Nelson, a ninety-year-old living legend. For the next ten minutes, I visited with him and his wife. We talked about the church, about Jesus, and about golf. And that was the highlight of my day.

You see, it's one thing to play the course; it's another thing to know the course designer. Regardless of how prestigious your church is, how rich its history, or how immaculate its grounds, there's something more important: Are you deeply acquainted with its Designer? It's one thing to preach; it's another to know the Word. It's one thing to lead the praise; it's another to abide with the King. It's one thing to offer the cup during the Lord's Supper; it's another to experience the One who offered his blood. Knowing the Designer is crucial to our ministries, because it's impossible to lead our people where we have never been.

The problem is that our lengthy to-do lists sometimes cause God to be put on hold. When we do choose to include him in our schedules, we have a tendency to hurry our awareness and rush our prayers so we can check off another task.

But was it a chore for me to visit with Byron Nelson for ten minutes? Was I constantly glancing at my watch, saying, "OK, hurry up. I need to move on"? Of course not! I was in the presence of the designer of the course, and because I love golf, I had already come to appreciate him.

Years ago I heard a preacher build a Christmas sermon around the fact that, when God left heaven to come to earth, there was no room for him in the inn. The message was titled "The Crowded-Out Christ." That title can describe the evaporating spiritual life of the hurried preacher. The challenge is to be certain that the demands of people don't take priority over finding a quiet place for Christ in our daily schedule.

—DS

What's on Your Mind?

A simple Secret:
Good leaders keep the big three leadership concepts constantly in mind.

The church is God's enterprise in the world, his "business," if you will. And there have been times we haven't taken care of business because we've failed to lead effectively. Perhaps it's because many of us still need to learn a crucial secret: In order to take care of the business entrusted to us, we need to spend a part of each day dealing with concepts that most heavily influence business success. Here are the big three:

Vision—Whether you lead a mom-and-pop ice-cream stand or an undertaking like ministry, part of your job is to understand and communicate the vision.

Understanding the vision requires that you constantly ask, *Where are we going? What are we seeking? What do we hope to accomplish here, now and in the future?* People are looking for someone wise and discerning to lead, and they count on these good leaders to give direction, to say, "This is where we are going." We would do well to devote part of our time to discerning and envisioning the destination. "If the trumpet does not sound a clear call," says the Apostle Paul, then "who will get ready for battle?" (1 Corinthians 14:8).

For years I taught that vision is a clear, compelling, magnetic image of a preferable future. I had heard the idea at some seminar, and it sounded right. However, I've come to realize that vision is more like a compass than a road map. It involves glimpsing the future and setting one's direction in light of that glimpse. Having vision is saying, "We are going east, not west, because this is what we have seen. We don't know all the details, we still need to pursue the plans, but we *are* going east. And that's enough—for now."

"Go as far as you can see," said Zig Ziglar, "and when you get there you will always be able to see farther."

Bottom-Line Utilization—I meet plenty of people who have tremendous vision, great dreams, and inspiring plans, but it is the rare individual who can back dreams with action. Do you have the ability to support your vision with meaningful action that makes full use of the raw materials at hand?

Sometimes supporting your vision is an exercise in reality-based reasonableness. Let's suppose you are the youth minister in a congregation of two hundred members. Let's also suppose that this congregation is in a town where the number of high school and middle school students is five hundred. And let's suppose that you say to your youth coaches that your youth ministry is going to grow from eleven students to five hundred students in one year. That is a marvelous vision, but what will enable you to see those results...beyond your words and the posters you create with your vision imprinted on them? In other words, the most effective leaders not only have great vision but they also have the resources to realize that vision.

Succession—We have dreams to pursue and resources to utilize, but we also have people to mentor. We must make sure that others who are well-equipped to lead will be following in our footsteps after we've moved on. It's a crucial aspect of the effective leader's responsibility—preparing, assisting, and nurturing the leaders of tomorrow.

I am convinced that if I were to die tomorrow, the ministry of Life-Bridge would be set back for about fifteen minutes (because some people would stop what they were doing in order to send my family flowers). There are effective people on board who can continue our ministry; none of us is irreplaceable. Our leadership team has even created a succession plan for use if an unforeseen emergency arises. But whether or not we face an emergency, we're still in the process of cultivating tomorrow's leaders.

So there you have it: vision, bottom-line utilization, and succession. If the church really is God's enterprise in the world, then we are his entrepreneurs. And with the attitude of a good business leader, we'll keep those Big Three Concepts constantly in mind.

—RR

Conflicted?

A simple Secret:
Worse than *having* conflict is *avoiding* conflict.

L ike most of us, you're probably not the kind of person who walks up to a fight on the street and asks, "Is this private, or can anyone jump in?" You prefer not to be in conflict. Ever.

Yet avoiding conflict is often more detrimental than choosing to move through it to resolution. And regardless of how conflict arises, we pastors are expected to initiate a resolution process. Resolving conflict begins by remembering that people tend to respond to conflict in one of four primary ways. Understanding how you and the other person respond can help you both reach a resolution.

Assert: "My way or the highway." These folks assert their authority and attempt to dominate, regardless of the situation. They respond to any disagreement by communicating that they are the sole owners of the right way: "When I want your opinion, I will give it to you."

• If it's them: When in conflict with these people, ask them to help you understand *why* they view the issue as they do. Ask permission to share your perspective. Usually an assertive person can be reasonable after the initial emotion has died down.

• If it's you: If you respond to conflict in this way, recognize that you need to back down a bit. Even after you think you've eased up considerably, drop it down another gear; you are usually just getting started at being reasonable!

Attack: "Not only is your idea wrong, but your mother is ugly." When feeling threatened, this person's response is to attack the other *person* rather than the problem.

• If it's them: Recognize that the individual who attacks is taking your comments personally. Make sure this person understands that you value him or her. Then work together to objectify the issue. Envision the process as placing the problem on a table in front of you, as if it's a project you are both working on through mutual cooperation.

• If it's you: If you attack in response to conflict, remember that most people are not attacking you when they disagree with one of your ideas. Take time to cool down and see the "innocence" of the other person's motivations. She is doing the best she can, although she may not be expressing herself in the most pleasing manner. Look for the core of the person's basic desire, which will be much like yours: wanting what's best for this church.

Avoid: "You won't be seeing me in church for a while." These folks put off, for as long as possible, any chance of directly facing a conflict. The problem with this approach is that issues simmer too long, then problems boil over and cause even more problems.

• If it's them: Reach out to these folks by taking the first steps in restoring fellowship. Do it gently and in a nonthreatening manner. Go to them as a sign of your sincere humility before the Lord. (You're a servant, remember?) Usually they'll respond in kind.

• If it's you: Don't wait until things come to a boiling point before making contact. "Nipping it in the bud" makes sense (unless you enjoy dealing with fully blossomed crises).

Acquiesce: "No problem, I can live with that." What these people are really thinking is "You are a jerk and always get your way." These people give in when they shouldn't. Then they let their anger simmer.

· If it's them: Help these people tell you what they really think by making sure they know you are "safe." Help them feel confident that you won't counter-attack and that you certainly won't reveal a confidence.

· If it's you: If you have a tendency to always give in, you need to recognize that disagreement does not necessarily mean lack of peace. Don't walk away wishing you had voiced your opinion.

As you discern the conflict styles, you and your partner in conflict can begin moving through the troubled landscape together by taking four basic steps: (1) identifying and clarifying the issue, (2) pursuing full understanding of the problem while agreeing to reserve judgement, (3) seeking and negotiating a compromise that benefits everyone, and (4) seeking mediation if you reach an impasse. Sometimes an issue simply cannot be resolved without a third party's help. Don't be afraid to allow that to happen.

Remember that it's possible to continue a relationship without reaching a resolution. You can walk hand in hand without seeing eye to eye. Or, as we often must say in the church, we don't have to be twins to be brothers.

—RR

Heading Toward the Vision?

A simple Secret:
Any road will do when you don't know where you're headed.

After a few trips, I discovered some important truths about Walt Disney World. Things seem real there, but they're not. The rides seem risky, but they're actually quite safe. And while Main Street USA is the epitome of idyllic existence...they make you go home at the end of the day.

We live in a real world. And we church leaders must cast a vision of what God can do in and through our people to make a lasting difference in this world.

How do we cast the vision? Try these three steps:

1. Acknowledge past achievements. We make a huge mistake if we assume we're the first to have taken some risks, created a challenge, or had a bold vision for the future. When we can find ways to celebrate the past without anchoring ourselves to it, we can begin to move forward.

Find ways to express gratitude for the people of faith and boldness who laid the groundwork so that you can move toward the future. Celebrate the fact that you sit under shade trees you didn't plant. For example, ask some of the old-timers to tell what it was like "way back when"; retell the history of the church on special occasions, describing the high points; invite former staff members back to celebrate their ministries (be wise here—no need to dredge up painful memories). Even when difficulties dot the timeline of the church, and even if you came to a troubled situation, you gain more credibility when you allow people to acknowledge that others, too, faced challenges, had faith, and took risks.

2. Clarify the needs of the present. According to Max DePree, "Good leaders define reality." Your job, then, is to help people see the current realities: This is where we are today; these are the challenges we'll face tomorrow. There are some hurdles to overcome, some problems to be addressed. Now.

In John 5, Jesus asks the man lying by the pool of Bethesda if he wants to get well. What a strange question to ask a man who has been unable to walk for almost forty years! It almost seems rude. But it is a great question, the same one Jesus is constantly asking our churches. If we answer in the affirmative, then some change will be necessary. What we have grown accustomed to doing we may not be able to continue to do. Our circle of friends will probably change. If we get well, our lives will never be the same.

I meet plenty of people and consult with many organizations. Many of them say they want to be well *but are not willing to change the things they're doing.* This is when pastors must gently but firmly assert the reality of the present.

3. Create a compelling image of the future. Vision has the power to raise our sights above the present reality and give us something better to shoot for. It has the power to inspire, motivate, and challenge, and it should have the power to drive us to our knees seeking God's strength and blessing. If our dreams are achievable through our own strength, then they are not God-sized dreams. Thus we prayerfully continue to raise the questions: What will our church look like tomorrow? How could it look in the coming year? in five years? Vision has the ability to take us away from the present and put us into the future.

According to a Chinese proverb, "If we keep heading in the same direction, we are likely to get where we are headed." When you look at the direction you or your congregation is heading, do you like where it is taking you? If you don't, why are you heading that way? Are you hoping for some intervention that will drastically alter your course? Are you counting on pure chance to save the day for you?

There is a wonderful scene in *Alice in Wonderland* in which Alice comes to a fork in the road. She asks the Cheshire Cat which way she should go.

The Cat notes that the answer "depends a good deal on where you want to get to."

Alice replies, "I don't much care where."

To which the cat says, "Then it doesn't matter which way you walk."

—RR

45 Two Simple Steps—That's It!

A simple Secret:
Developing leaders is difficult—but not complicated.

Churches often experience three phases with their ministers:

1. "Blessed is he who comes in the name of the Lord."

2. "By what authority are you doing these things?"

3. "Crucify him! Crucify him!"

As church leaders, we certainly have the opportunity to make a difference in the life of a church, to provide leadership and pastoral care, to feed, guide, and comfort; those responsibilities are all part of the ministry. We're also supposed to be developing more leaders.

Finding and developing leaders can be a challenge for us. Why? Because we've found that sometimes it's just easier to do things ourselves. The problem with this approach is that there's usually more work than we can do on our own. Therefore, we'll need to develop additional leaders if we're going to improve and enlarge our ministry, year after year.

As I see it, developing leaders allows me to expand the talent pool and actually maximize my own giftedness. We each have strengths and we each have weaknesses, so finding others to help us in our areas of weakness can help us maximize our strengths. In addition, developing leaders means I'm building the church as Jesus called me to do. Naturally, he intends that the church be healthy, vibrant, and dynamic. As we help others discover their gifts and utilize them for kingdom work, we are encouraging that kind of church into existence.

So how do we, at our church, develop leaders in this wonderful cause? We think in terms of only two basic steps: We recruit, and we equip.

Carefully recruit them. We identify them. We know of their maturity, skills, or availability probably because we've observed them in another arena, such as work, school, or a church-related project. It's true that sometimes potential new leaders will do the initiating. They think of us. For whatever reason, they volunteer or look for an opportunity to serve and grow in responsibility. Either way, be cautious, because not everyone is ready for leadership. Many have taken on significant responsibilities and been overwhelmed or have quickly displayed their lack of maturity or skill. The rule is true in hiring volunteers, too: Hire slow, fire fast.

Equip them! Our church provides job descriptions and precise expectations for each job so that everyone is clearly on the same page. We also provide a one-year leadership institute. This institute covers spiritual growth, doctrinal issues, church vision and mission, and practical leadership training. We now require that individuals taking on a leadership role first go through the leadership institute. As John Maxwell has said, "There is only one thing worse than equipping leaders and losing them; it's not equipping them and keeping them."

That's it for the basics of leadership development. Difficult, but not complicated. Just remember that your job is to be a cheerleader, a vision caster, a mentor. You won't always get immediate, tangible results; it takes time to develop people. One of the keys is to make sure you give authority as well as responsibility. As the leader, ultimately you have the responsibility. But do learn to delegate that authority.

—RR

There's No I in *Team*

A simple Secret:
Allegiance and teamwork thrive in the arena of encouragement.

Years ago the noted English architect Sir Christopher Wren was supervising the construction of a magnificent cathedral in London. A journalist thought it would be interesting to interview some of the workers, so he chose three and asked them, "What are you doing?"

The first replied, "I'm cutting stone for ten shillings a day."

The next answered abruptly, "What's it look like I'm doing? I'm breaking up these rocks for this job."

But the third said, "I have the distinct privilege of helping Sir Christopher Wren construct one of London's greatest cathedrals."

If you serve as an associate or assistant minister, you are vitally important. Associates don't always sense their worth, however. I am thankful that the senior pastors I've served with have always shared the spotlight and even, at times, taken the hits for me. It's my hope that all of us have an opportunity to enjoy such a spirit of humility and teamwork with our bosses. What helps a senior pastor and his associates work as a team? Here are some important team-building attitudes to develop:

Resist the allure of titles. In the kingdom of God, you never rise higher than the position of a servant. Whether or not you are the big cheese, lead dog, or head hog at the trough, go out of your way to let your associates know that you aren't wrapped up in titles. Titles are fleeting; testimonies are lasting.

Take the focus off yourself. If you're in authority, shine the spotlight on your staff. When you catch someone doing something right, commend him or her both privately and publicly. Your words of reinforcement carry more weight than you may realize. Most of us can go for a long time on one sincere compliment.

Think *we* rather than *me*. As the senior leader, embrace the philosophy that it doesn't matter who gets the credit. This will assure all team members that they do fill a distinctive purpose within the organization. While someone has said that the toughest instrument to play in the orchestra is second fiddle, the sky is the limit for the assistant. Let each one know that God will use his or her humility as a tool for both evangelism and unity.

Appreciate all those utility players. (Also known as volunteers!) These individuals are skilled in more than one position. When a need arises, they step in and fill the void. Their labors may bring success to the entire team, including the coach.

Glorify God and edify your superior. Whether you are the senior pastor or the associate, remember that you both serve the same Master. If you cannot support and encourage one another, then the kingdom may be better served if you were in another setting.

First Corinthians 12 masterfully outlines the spirit of teamwork that should permeate every church. We have different functions but together form one body. Use your role to glorify Christ, making certain that if anyone gets the credit, it's him. Thus you'll begin to see your ministry as much more than a job; you'll realize that it is a distinct privilege.

—DS

Personal and Spiritual Growth

Gather the Guides

A simple Secret:
Learn what you need to know by staying close to those in the know.

Y ou don't know what you don't know. And you don't realize what you don't know until you discover that what you *do* know isn't enough.

I would like to believe that when I was younger I had the good sense to know I didn't know what I needed to know. The reality is that I stumbled onto an amazingly effective habit that has been of great benefit to me: gathering "knowers" around me.

Since my early days in college, certain people have been influential as knowledgeable mentors in my life. I invited each of them to tell me freely what I needed to know. The first few were good people who, either because I asked or as some personal project (penance) on their part, allowed me to tag along with them. This wasn't an organized, systematic, in-depth program. Rather, these folks let me travel with them to speaking engagements or invited me to board meetings or luncheons. Sometimes they invited me to their homes.

The point is, I knew they knew stuff I didn't know. So hanging with them gave me the opportunity to see how they worked and how they behaved. I was able to see what kinds of things they deemed important and how they drew those conclusions. Those early impressions were important to me, and ever since those days, I've intentionally gathered mentors around me.

Are you doing the same? There are people around you ready to take you under their wings. Here's how you could approach the whole idea of inviting someone to influence your life.

Over lunch or some other informal meeting, ask your potential mentor if he or she would be willing to set aside a regular time to meet with you. You might decide upon once a week, once a month, or sometimes even less regularly, depending on the person and your schedules.

In your initial meetings, ask your mentor to provide insight, direction, correction, or whatever he or she believes you need. I've found that my mentors will ask me what I want to know. My response is always the same: I don't know the specifics. I want to know what *they* know, and I'm not sure what that is.

In addition, I establish some basic ground rules. Mentors can tell me anything they want, without judgment from me. They will find it difficult to hurt my feelings for long, so if there is something I need to hear, then I want them to tell me. *I really do want to know what they know.*

Early on, you'll likely need to "prime the pump." I've found questions like these to be useful in getting things going:

What have you read lately that proved interesting and beneficial?

How do you make decisions?

What has been your greatest success?

What has been your biggest disappointment?

What would you do differently if you had the chance?

What do you dream about?

What has helped you the most to grow spiritually?

What have you done to compensate for weaknesses?

How have you maximized your strengths?

When have you experienced your deepest satisfactions in life?

Why have you chosen the path(s) that you have chosen?

Who has influenced you the most—and how?

What do you think I need to know that I don't know?

What do you perceive as my greatest need at the moment?

Each year I've invited someone new to act as my mentor (and thanked the person who took time with me during the previous year). I've absorbed priceless nuggets of wisdom on relationships, business, money, ministry, success, opportunity, failure, faith—the list is nearly endless. Some of the advice has been profound, some quite down-to-earth. Sometimes the mentoring has been deeply spiritual and at other times quite practical. And I've formed some wonderful friendships with business people, lawyers, custodians, mechanics, doctors, ministers, and a host of others who have helped me discover what I didn't know—what I really *needed* to know.

—RR

Bear Stickers

A simple Secret:
Little things can remind you of big truths.

He was running a little late for lunch, and I was afraid he might have changed his mind about getting together after all. It had been quite awhile since he'd moved to this southern state, coming to heal, to repair relationships, and to be reconciled to his calling. I had prayed for him, often having been instructed by him in so many ways.

I was speaking at a conference in the area where he now lived, and we'd decided to meet. It was an easy decision, because he had been a mentor from a distance and occasionally up close. Nearly thirty years older than I, he had built a greatly admired ministry, had strong preaching skills, and had provided leadership for all kinds of national ministries. He had spoken numerous times at my college, and since I'd graduated he was one of the men I had looked to for leadership. In so many ways he was a giant of a man.

But he had made the mistake of breaking his vows to his wife and was asked to resign. The ensuing mess was difficult for all involved. You know the drill when a leader messes up like this: Some come to his support, some come to crucify. Some ignore a long friendship. Some can relate. Some cannot imagine. Many avoid.

Now he and his wife had been invited to a place where they might repair things, learn and be challenged, work at healing their hearts. It was a good place and a gracious invitation. I was looking forward to getting together for lunch.

He walked in a little out of breath, carrying a small display case. He was working at a sales job, and one of his appointments had run a little long. It was good to see him. We talked about the weather and his job and the restaurant's special-of-the-day. I told him I was glad he had come.

He told me it had been a difficult trip. Then he shared the ache of his heart and the disappointment of his choices. He challenged me to be smart, to watch my steps, and to guard against temptation. We cried some and laughed some and prayed some. I had come to encourage; he had come to share. And we both grew a little wiser.

Too soon his sales appointments beckoned. But before he left he opened his display case and offered me some little bear stickers. His current employer specialized in putting a company's name on little gadgets: magnets, golf balls, hats, bear stickers. He thought my two boys would enjoy the stickers. Then he packed up and headed off to make a sale, pay his bills, and grow in grace. I watched him go. And it was sad to see him hurry off with his case of samples.

He was right. My boys loved the bear stickers. Aged three and five, they stuck those bear stickers on lots of things. One even ended up on my travel alarm.

I didn't pay much attention to that little sticker until several weeks later. I'd been traveling quite a bit, caught up in a whirlwind of airports, taxis, and hotels. Then one night I sat on the edge of the bed to set my alarm and actually noticed that bear sticker. I was reminded of the lessons I learned from the giant of a man who was now selling baubles from a briefcase.

For years that travel alarm went with me. Even after it had worn out. It was a reminder of how quickly a promise can be broken and how tragic the consequences can be—a reminder of how important our promises are and a reminder that, but for the grace of God, I could be selling bear stickers too.

—RR

It's Worth It!

Ministry, with its myriad demands and hectic schedules, can sometimes be discouraging. And so often it's the people part of what we do that takes the greatest toll on our hopeful spirits. I once heard an elderly pastor speaking to a group of seminary students. He said, "Ministry is wonderful because of the people, and ministry is difficult because of the people."

How can people bring both pain and blessing? Some folks are wonderful simply because they work at it. Some are natural encouragers, and some have experienced such changed hearts that they become perpetually grateful. Some of the difficult people are that way because of personal tragedy or disappointment. Others seem just plain mean by temperament. Harvard professor Benjamin Zander said, "A cynic, after all, is a passionate person who does not want to be disappointed again." Isn't this the case with many of the people in our congregations? But the point is, if you're in ministry you know that people can be a blessing or a curse and sometimes both—no matter how they arrived at their current state.

> To dwell above with the saints I love,
> Oh, that will be glory.
> But to live below with the saints I know,
> Well, that's another story.
> *(author unknown)*

We know that we'll all be perfected someday and spend an eternity together in relational bliss. Until then, however, we must proceed with earthly ministry, recognizing that it's not for the faint of heart. In fact, ministry can be downright devastating for many. At those times, nothing much will help except a good sabbatical, an extended retreat, or some professional counseling. For example, our church utilizes a place called Blessing Ranch in Livermore, Colorado. Dr. John Walker and his staff specialize in assisting ministers in renewal and restoration. Any of us can benefit from such a spiritual and emotional health checkup occasionally.

For those less difficult times, I've found a secret. It began when I was a junior in college, and I call it my "It's Worth It" box. In this box I place every encouraging card, letter, and note I've received throughout the years. Some of them express gratitude for my ministry; others offer words of personal encouragement. Still others simply remind me that it is God who has called me to ministry—and that he is always at my side.

I keep that box in my office, and when the going gets especially tough, I reach inside it. The reassuring words are often an antidote to a particularly tough day or situation. I'm instantly transported back to people, places, and events that have made ministry so worthwhile over the years.

I now have several "It's Worth It" boxes after twenty-plus years in ministry. I don't really know why I haven't pitched some of the old ones, but I tend to hang on to things. Maybe there will be a day when some dusty, yellowed letter will be a refreshing reminder to an old man that it really has been worth it, after all.

—RR

The "Place" of Prayer

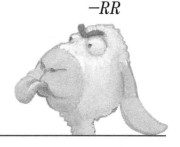

A simple Secret:
When it comes to prayer, think, location, location, location!

Preachers do a great deal of praying in the sanctuary—especially during the special music, just before the sermon! While God hears the cry of the panicked, he's more likely to bless a more intentional effort. And sometimes our intentions will be made clearer when we choose a location that more directly connects us to the person or cause on our hearts. If the idea is new to you, consider these two points.

First, the church is bigger than the pulpit area—so why not take the time and effort to pray in various locations and seats throughout the sanctuary on the night before the service? You have your own key; use it! Come to the church when you know others won't be there. Move throughout the rows, praying specifically for the people who may be sitting there the next day. Since people are creatures of habit, sometimes you will know exactly for whom you are praying. Simply ask God to open their hearts to his Word. Pray that people will respond to the Spirit's calling.

Several years ago, after I'd prayed in several locations for specific people, a fifty-five-year-old banker with heart problems responded to the invitation and committed his life to Christ. I know we are to pray confidently, expecting the Lord to give us the desires of our hearts; nevertheless, I was a bit stunned. As I hugged the man, I said, "I was praying for you last night." While I don't recall his reply, I do remember a gentle divine chiding: "Oh, ye of little faith."

Similar situations have occurred time and time again, but please don't misunderstand me. There's nothing magical about where we're sitting when we pray. What does matter is this simple truth: With God all things are possible (Matthew 19:26). Prayer unleashes God's power, and most sanctuaries I've been in could use a little more power! The location can help connect us, physically and emotionally, to what we're seeking spiritually.

Second, realize that this simple secret of "location praying" need not be relegated to the church sanctuary. For best results, try it throughout your church and community. Drive-by shootings had been in the news in our area, so we decided to try Ted Haggard's Christian alternative of "drive-by praying." Our staff and elders filled several cars and headed out from the church parking lot. For a solid hour, the only things we said aloud were sentence prayers. It quickly became apparent that this would be a moving experience for everyone in each car. The time flew. We prayed for people walking along the streets, for specific neighborhoods. We prayed outside bars and within churches. That evening, in sixty minutes' time, ten carloads covered our entire community in prayer.

Pray without ceasing sounds like a pretty strong admonition, but what a mindset to cultivate! Sometimes prayer changes things; usually prayer changes us. And what's the worst thing that could happen if you become a little creative in choosing your place of prayer? A church member might catch you down on your knees, fervently praying for your flock. If word got out, it could start a revival and transform your church. So pray...in the sanctuary, along the sidewalk, and in your Subaru.

—DS

51 The Benefit of a Day Off

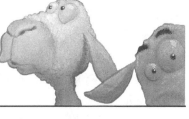

A simple Secret:
When you schedule rest, you *and* your people benefit.

To put it mildly, the minister has a rather unique schedule. Your Christmas season overflows with special programs, parties, and Christmas Eve services. Easter season to the minister is like April is to an accountant. And your demanding schedule doesn't stop there. Year in and year out, you work weekends. Contrary to what a handful of spiritual couch potatoes in your church may say, you *do* work more than one day a week!

One of the challenges of life in the ministry is being on call 24/7. In the Ten Commandments, God included the concept of a Sabbath day's rest for a very good reason. While it's tough for some ministers to take a break from the grind of ministry, it's healthy for both you and your flock in the long run. Follow these tips, and your day off will be just that—a day off.

• Prepare by enlisting lay leaders to help you have a day off. Recruit some of your key lay leaders to help shoulder the responsibility of covering hospital calls and small emergencies that will arise on your day off. The church will be strengthened by this, and the volunteers will grow from it. (After all, even the Lone Ranger had Tonto.)

• Ask your secretary to contact you on your cell phone if an emergency arises. (This is one more reason to allow only a handful of people to have your cell-phone number.)

• Screen your phone calls at home with an answering machine. In the case of an emergency, you can take the call or return it as soon as you get the message. If it isn't an emergency, it isn't fair to your family or to yourself to do today what you can put off until tomorrow.

• Make certain your voice mail greeting is different on your day off so that callers don't expect an immediate call back. Then check your voice mail messages at the end of your day off. Better yet, don't check your voice mail until the next day.

• Once a month, take your day off *out of town* where you won't run into your church members. Bob Russell refers to this practice as "getting out of the area code." This protects the Sabbath as a day of rest and keeps members from continually bringing to you the things that can wait.

Take your day off! That is the most important tip. For several years I prided myself on only occasionally doing so, but over time this approach took its toll. What I thought to be dedication to the ministry was really foolishness and pride.

According to an Indian proverb, "You will break the bow if you always keep it bent." When your ministry becomes an obsession instead of a profession, your family will always get the short end of the stick. But when you nurture the habit of taking that day off, rest assured that Someone wants to refresh and renew you. He promises, "Come to me, all you who are weary and burdened, and I will give you rest."

—DS

52 Keep the Worship Embers Glowing Bright

A simple Secret:
As you keep telling the story, grow closer to its Hero.

It's quite easy for us to tell the story so often that we forget to hear it ourselves. Then we fail to let it have the ongoing, transforming effect on our hearts that it had when we responded to it the very first time. The gospel story, of course, was our first love as believers. But that love can grow lukewarm as we minister; it can even sink to the level of coldness. Sometimes the sacred story loses its romance for the ones who tell it so regularly.

One of the occupational hazards of ministry is that those of us who lead in worship can forget to be led. We shouldn't take any shortcuts here, though. Currently both Dave and I preach in places that have multiple services, and time is at a premium, as it likely is for you. Nevertheless, there are some things any of us can do to ensure our own opportunities to worship. Here are a few ideas we've tried (but bear in mind that neither of us do all these things, nor do we assume that this is the be-all and end-all of ways to enhance your personal worship):

• We make sure that we attend at least one of our churches' multiple services in its entirety.

• We set aside time during the week for our own personal worship. I have discovered that listening to worship music and tapes of other ministers is quite helpful during this time.

• Before the services, we pray with all involved. We pray not only that we will *lead* in worship but also that we will be *led* in worship.

• We've each joined a study group that we *don't* lead. It need not be a group within our own congregation. We have a friend who gets together with other local ministry people for study. He has discovered two benefits from this: He is spiritually fed, and he has the opportunity to interact with other denominational perspectives.

• We meet regularly with staff members for a time of worship. My church's staff has a devotional time each Wednesday morning. We worship, pray, and discuss as we work our way through a section of Scripture.

• We've each found a retreat designed for ministry people that is focused on personal worship (not simply another "how-to" conference).

• We record how the story continues to influence our lives—and we make sure the people around us know we celebrate that.

My church gives each full-time member of our ministry staff six weekends a year, in addition to designated vacation time, free from responsibilities. Staff members are encouraged to visit other churches, spend the time with their families, and just use the "space" to rest from being a leader every weekend. It's important because, if we're not careful, the story we love—that old, old precious story—can become too familiar to our hearts. When that happens, we'll have difficulty conveying it with all the deep, heartfelt passion it deserves.

—RR

Where's the Passion?

A simple Secret:
First look at the carpet.

I was speaking at a team-building seminar for a company that manufactures carpet-cleaning equipment. The company had brought together hundreds of its national and international distributors for the annual meeting, and I had arrived early to get a feel for the crowd. The speakers preceding me were carpet-cleaning experts, imparting all the latest information on carpet care and restoration. The participants were hungry for the information and cheered each new development.

It was impressive to see so much passion for something I'd always taken for granted. After all, carpet isn't exactly glamorous, and cleaning and caring for it isn't on everyone's list of the most exciting vocations. Yet, for these people, it apparently held the key to the meaning of the universe.

And before I knew it, I was fired up too! The adrenaline began to flow, and it was all about...clean carpet.

What hooked me? It certainly wasn't carpet itself or knowing the differences in thread weight and backing. It wasn't the various new concoctions providing easier cleaning, nor was it understanding how to increase the wear factor. What hooked me was the participants' absolute commitment to carpet.

Their enthusiasm for their business was astounding. On my drive home I found myself wondering whether people left our church services knowing how passionate I am about the gospel message. I wondered whether they knew my absolute commitment to Christ's cause. I thought about whether our church conveys our love of God and his fantastic, historic announcement for sinners.

It struck me how unenthusiastic we preachers and teachers can appear to be. Perhaps we have allowed the old, old story to become just that—an old, old story. We seem to forget what God has done for us. In too many churches, we sit and listen, or stand and preach, then politely head for our cars, and no difference seems to have been made.

If we are not careful, we fail to recognize or remember just how powerful is the message of Christ. We establish our routines, we set our watches by what happens in a service, and we take that which is extraordinary and make it seem rather ordinary. Yet my carpet-cleaning friends *had taken something ordinary and made it the most important thing in the world.*

No, you don't have to jump around in the aisles or orchestrate a standing ovation to allow your passion to shine through. But you may need to discard a few worn-out routines to communicate the old story in fresh ways.

Along those lines, here's a little suggestion. The next time you step up to the pulpit, look down at the carpet. For a brief moment, let your imagination wrap itself around an amazing image: Somewhere in the world there's a group of men and women bouncing around like crazed little puppies. With full-throated enthusiasm, they're yelling and clapping and laughing. They've just heard about a tough old stain that will no longer stand up to a brand-new miracle detergent. For them, it's the kingdom come.

When it comes to our own tough stain—our sin problem, which has eternal consequences—there's some pretty good news too...

Can you feel your heart beating a little faster?

—RR

Professional Development

Don't Waste That Workshop!

A simple Secret:
Conventions and seminars can have ongoing influence.

You enjoyed nearly every minute of it—creative ideas, new programs, the latest trends. You left inspired to do more, be more, and see more results. You were boosted spiritually and motivated out of your socks. So how is it that a few months after the convention you've forgotten or barely used so much of what you heard?

Several years ago I decided to do something about this unhappy phenomenon. I decided to skip conventions and seminars that year and, instead, take time to review my notes and tapes from programs I'd attended previously. I was surprised at all the great (and untried) ideas tucked away in those copious notes, and I determined to start making the most of the events I'd attend in the future. If that's your desire, as well, here's what I suggest:

· Before choosing your seminars for the year, make a list of personal and ministry needs. In what areas would you like some help?

· Carefully research an event you might attend. Does it offer any of the things you need? Will it address the specific issues you've identified?

· Prepare by reading the books and materials of the various speakers and presenters. Check out their Web sites, too.

· Take with you as many co-workers or volunteers as you can. Plan to attend different workshops and then get together to swap notes. Relax and enjoy each other and take time to brainstorm about what you're hearing. How could it apply at your church?

· After the session, try to speak with the presenter. Ask specific questions. If you are bold enough, ask whether he or she might be free to meet for a few minutes over coffee or lunch. In this way you'll occasionally be able to receive one-on-one guidance.

• Ask the presenter for specific ways his or her ideas have worked in real life. What were some of the difficulties? How have the programs worked in other places? Some of the best insights I've gleaned from presenters have come in response to these questions. Often finding out what *hasn't* worked— or what significant problems arose—can be the best information you'll hear.

• After you've returned to the office, organize the notes and ideas in a format you can easily use. Just keeping the notebooks on your shelves or creating a file for them probably won't accomplish much for you. Learn to break the information into smaller parts so you can locate specific ideas as related needs arise.

• Within the first week after the convention or seminar, get together with co-workers or volunteers to discuss the highlights of what you heard. This can be a great opportunity to include others in thinking about *how* they are doing *what* they are doing.

• Don't assume that what worked in a presenter's church will work for you. Consider the differing demographics and psychographics of your situation. Also take into account what the presenter did to prepare his or her congregation for the endeavor.

• If you do decide to implement a new program or idea, be wise about introducing it. Scope the issue; list pros and cons. Anticipate the hurdles, and elicit buy-in by allowing people to have input on the front end. Do all the things you would do if this were your idea from scratch—and be flexible as you truly share the power.

• Schedule a block of time ninety days after the seminar or convention to review your notes and ideas. This will force you to keep some of the good things you heard in front of you.

• If the ideas you gleaned inspire you to undertake a major shift, call people who are further into the process. Get their insights, which will flow from hands-on experience.

Conventions and seminars can have ongoing influence for the good. They remind us of what we need to be doing, and sometimes they simply encourage us to keep going. If we consider how much we spend to attend and factor in the cost of our time, though, it's a shame not to use the things we learned.

—RR

Ready for Risk?

A simple Secret:
Until you're free to fail, you won't be free to succeed.

What would you attempt if you knew you couldn't fail? Fear of failure is one of life's greatest fears. If we knew our attempts would be successful, we'd eagerly pursue our fondest aspirations and quickly embark on every voyage prompted by our dreams. Our fear stops us from beginning, from dreaming, from venturing too far from the comfort zone.

However, unless we're open to the possibility of failure, we remain closed to opportunities for success. Until we allow that failure could happen and move forward in spite of that possibility, we may never know accomplishment.

Let's suppose I wasn't sure whether I could move from standing to walking. Instead, I simply stood in place hanging tightly to a rail. I might dream about walking, listen to motivational tapes about walking, read books on walking, join a small group for walking enthusiasts...but until I let go of the rail and take a step, *I will never know if I can walk.* Until I am free to fail, I am not free to succeed. (As someone once said, "You'll never stub your toe standing still.")

Of course, none of this means we ought to avoid planning, refuse to consider all the consequences, or take reckless leaps into thin air. It simply means that—after due consideration and wise preparation—we must be free to fail if we are going to be free to succeed.

As you think about the future of your ministry, what are some of your dreams? And what are you doing about those dreams? When you look over your plans and your budget, do they include anything that might be risky? Or do they only represent what is safe, what has already proven to be feasible? The point is, if we'd be foolish only to plan unproven efforts, so also are we foolish to plan only what's guaranteed to be pain free.

Jesus condemned the one-talent man (see Matthew 25), not for his failure, but for his lack of effort. The fact is, the man had taken what he'd been given and came back to the master saying, "I'm returning this to you, safe and sound." The attitude angered the master because the servant had been given both means and opportunity. He had plenty of options and yet did nothing but dig a hole deep enough to keep the talent safe.

We could envision this man sitting in his recliner with a bag of chips and the remote, confident he had done what was needed. The master returned, and the one-talent man stood in line, proudly waiting to demonstrate his zealous avoidance of risk. He hadn't lost that talent, but the master didn't see anything laudable in that fact. He saw squandered opportunity, wasted talent, and lazy effort.

I am convinced that if the one-talent man had attempted some investment, used his talent and lost it, he would have received the same blessing the others received. Safety first isn't always the best option.

—RR

The Courage to Encourage

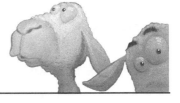

A simple Secret:
Hey, guys, it's not a competition!

Perhaps it's understandable that church leaders often view other church leaders as "the competition." But don't fall for this. We're all co-laborers working for the common good of the kingdom. Our sermons contain admonitions to affirm one another. We wax eloquent on our responsibility to encourage. But somehow we intend this for "the laity" and not for ourselves. What a tragedy!

It's true that crossing denominational lines and setting aside opportunities to be with other ministers takes time, but it's worth the effort. Our church invites every minister from our area to attend a quarterly prayer luncheon. On those days I'm seated at a round table with Christian brothers and sisters who lead in other congregations. We eat, laugh, and pray for one another. Our sharing goes deeper than typical social conversations. Here we lean on one another and reveal our disappointments, as well as our victories.

But if our interaction is relegated to four ninety-minute segments a year, we miss out on the real power of deeper relationships. Consider this story I heard about my brother Jeff.

Jeff truly has both a kindness and a kingdom-consciousness. Recently, at a Christian convention, I heard another minister share about one of Jeff's extra-mile efforts to undergird him. The speaker said, "A few years ago, we were going through a very challenging transition at our church, and it was a dark night of the soul for me, personally. Jeff Stone, who ministers in a suburb several hours away, called me and asked how I was doing. At the time I didn't know Jeff all that well, but he'd heard about our situation from my children's director when they both attended another conference. Jeff asked if he could drive up, take me to lunch, and pray with me. I was floored. The next day, that's exactly what he did. He closed our time together by laying his hands on me and praying for me and my ministry. And when I thanked him for taking a day to do this, he casually said, 'You would have done the same thing for me.' "

The speaker concluded his story: "It was gut-check time. I was honest with him, and I said, 'Jeff, I wouldn't have driven those hours to pray with you.' "

Then he said to the audience, "But, friends, I will now. That's the lesson God taught me—that we can mature to the point of not secretly smiling when other ministers hit hard times. Instead, we can embrace them and help them on the journey."

—DS

57 Advance by Retreating

A simple Secret:
Getting away with your staff will refresh your ministry.

The longer you provide life-giving water to others, the quicker your own "well" can run dry. Over time, all the lessons, talks, counseling sessions, and sermons can sap your energy and drain your creativity.

Not even our Lord could minister without periods of rest and communion with the Father.

Jesus withdrew from the crowds to pray by himself when he needed strength. At other times he retreated from the throng in order to be with his disciples. There is a lesson for every minister in his examples. If the Son of God needed a respite from the demands of people, then how much more do we and the people we work with?

In order to keep moving forward, we all need to pull over sometimes and get refreshed at a spiritual rest area. Several times a year, try to follow Christ's lead and pull away from the masses with your staff. Allow yourselves time to learn from and encourage one another.

Time spent away from the office to be with the Lord can energize you and your staff spiritually and professionally. A change of scenery can do wonders for your team. If you always meet in the same room at the same time, you will probably come up with the same ideas, same worship services, and same programs.

Leaving the confines of the church also allows you to remove distractions. In the church office, it's easy to become preoccupied with the to-do list on your desk or to overhear your secretary talking on the phone to a member who "just has to talk to you." But when you're off-site, such things fade into the background, ensuring that your meeting is guided by a compass rather than a clock. Such settings allow you the freedom to brainstorm and tweak the group's best ideas until you arrive at the decisions that point you in the right direction.

Your retreat need not be long; a day will do. And it need not be held at some faraway place or expensive property. Consider locations such as these:

• a church member's house that's secluded and has a large, comfortable room, enclosed porch, or backyard deck;

• a nearby camp or retreat center;

• a restaurant or country club with a private room;

• anywhere in Hawaii. (Hey, it's worth a try!)

The bottom line is that when you become so involved in the work of the Lord that you forget the Lord of the work, it's time for a retreat. (As pastor Rick Warren says, "If you burn the candle at both ends, you're probably not as bright as you think you are.") As strange as it may seem, sometimes the only way to advance is to retreat. In fact, you'll likely find that time spent alone with your staff becomes crucial to the success of your organization. Friendships will deepen. New ideas will bubble up. And your spiritual life together will freshen.

—DS

Start a "Smile File"

A simple Secret:
With humor, practice makes perfect.

A certain pastor was known for never being able to tell a funny story because he always forgot the punch line. One day he heard a conference speaker dramatically announce to his audience, "I have a confession to make to you today. Some of the happiest moments of my life have been spent in the arms of another man's wife."

The crowd gasped. The masterful speaker smiled and said, "My mother!" The audience erupted with laughter. And the pastor thought to himself, *Surely I can remember that punch line.* He knew his own church would love that joke.

So the next Sunday, the preacher began his message with a grave expression on his face, stared out at his congregation, and said, "I have a confession to make today. Some of the happiest moments of my life have been spent in the arms of another man's wife."

The crowd gasped and then became deathly quiet, but the preacher's mind had gone blank. He fidgeted. He began to sweat. He even tried to set up the punch line again, saying, "Some of the happiest moments of my life have been spent in the arms of another man's wife." Then he mumbled, "And for the life of me, I can't remember who she was!"

If that describes your own ability to tell a joke, then read on. Humor should relax your congregation, and it need not stress you out. Why is it that some preachers' jokes never bomb? The answer is simple: They save funny jokes they've heard, and they practice telling them. Here are a few tips to remember as you build your very own Smile File:

• Write down the good ones as you hear them. (Don't trust your memory.) Jot down the punch line and some key phrases that set up the joke.

• Keep your favorites where you can easily retrieve them. For example, create a document on your computer and label it "Smile File." Fill it with the jokes and stories you know are guaranteed to go over well. When a particular story will complement your message perfectly, cut and paste as needed.

• Plan to bounce each joke off of a handful of friends. The more you practice telling a joke, the more comfortable you'll feel about using it in a lesson or sermon. The more you practice telling a joke without notes in everyday situations, the less you'll need your notes when you deliver it to your congregation. It also gives you an opportunity to practice thinking on your feet, just in case—God forbid—the joke should bomb.

Just remember to tickle the funny bone in moderation. Jokes for the sake of entertainment rarely serve a purpose in the pulpit. But well-practiced humor with a purpose can pave the way for the gospel to penetrate a hardened heart.

—DS

Is Anyone Helping You Prepare?

A simple Secret:
You aren't the only one who can research a sermon.

Tony Campolo preached a sermon titled "It Was Friday but, Thank God, Sunday Is Coming!"—a marvelous message about hope in the Resurrection. But for some of us preachers, the preparation of an inspiring message suggests a different slant on that title: "It's Friday and—Oh, No!—Sunday Is Coming."

There are plenty of things on your plate, but one duty remains constant: weekly sermon prep. Sunday is over, and you can relax for a few moments. Then, all of sudden, it's time to prepare a new message. Keeping your sermons biblical, fresh, relevant, and understandable requires a fair amount of hard work.

But are you the only one who can do the work? Who among us doesn't regularly receive lists of suggested readings and e-mails with the latest round of heart-warming stories, cute jokes, and questionable Madelyn Murray O'Hair rumors? With all the willing contributors out there, we can create a research team that will read, sort, clip, and send material that we might find useful.

Simply invite people from your congregation (or an even broader pool of researchers) to be a part of this special team. Actually, virtually anyone could participate. Just provide a few guidelines to get your volunteers started, and you'll be on your way to more productive (and likely more relevant) sermon preparation.

• Provide an outline of sermon topics and themes as far into the future as you can—at least for the next few months. Be as specific as possible about the tack you are going to take, including the primary and ancillary Scripture passages you'll likely use.

• Ask your team members to provide a synopses of a book or to highlight passages in an article or newspaper clipping—anything that helps you get the main point without having to read the entire work.

• Ask researchers to label or categorize the material they are passing along. And make sure they include the source (author, publisher, date of publication, the exact quotation, and page numbers).

• Let your helpers know how valuable this ministry is to you, and also let them know that although you may never be able to directly use what they provide, it does assist you in sorting through many ideas as you prepare your messages.

• Let all participants know upfront that you won't be able to give them credit—that it's a behind-the-scenes ministry. (I've never known anyone who even *wanted* public recognition, though.) But don't forget to recognize them privately by sending a note telling them how much their contributions have helped you.

Along with making sure your group understands its tasks and responsibilities, you'll need to discipline yourself in some ways, as well. Here are some rules for you to live by as you begin using a research team.

• Create a file folder for each topic, and file the material you receive.

• Recognize that some folks will provide very useful things on a regular basis and that others will only occasionally hit the target. Either way you have a great starting place for ideas.

• Realize that some people will naturally gravitate to certain ideas or sources. One person on my team provides wonderful book synopses, while another provides jokes.

• Don't expect great results immediately. It will take some trial and error to teach people what to look for. Occasionally you'll need to gently quench someone's exuberance when he tries to convince you, for instance, to use the "Footprints in the Sand" poem because it's unique and unknown. Try to remain grateful for each suggestion, even if it's trite and overused. (You can help eliminate some of that by communicating specific guidelines and teaching researchers where to look for quality material.)

• Be assured that the attention span of a few people in the congregation will increase dramatically as team members listen intently each week to see if their suggestions are being used. Your attendance will increase, as well, as people who are researching for you become regular attendees. If you have more than one service, and you use researchers' recommendations, they may even attend the other services and bring their friends. *"Listen, right there— that was my idea!"*

—RR

Two Heads: Better Than One

A simple Secret:
Sermon improvement can be a group thing.

If two heads are better than one, then what about three or four when it comes to sermon preparation? I'm not advising you to just pick and choose from ideas that other people generate, nor am I suggesting that others write your sermons. The purpose isn't even to shorten your preparation time, although sometimes that may occur. Rather, a preaching study group is built on the premise that, ultimately, proclaiming the Word is a community responsibility and that the Holy Spirit is in the midst of us, not only individually but corporately. Thus there is great power in our fellowship as we study the Scriptures together and invite God's Spirit to lead us into a deeper understanding of his message to us.

Start by finding several ministers in your region who have a passion for preaching. When choosing who to invite, remember that God has gifted each of us differently. It is healthy to include people with strengths and styles that differ from ours. This allows "iron to sharpen iron" in creative, often unexpected ways.

Together, plan a sermon series or two for several months in advance, and commit to preaching on the same text. You'll work together on those texts each week. The format could work like this:

Wednesdays: Send an e-mail to the others, sharing an outline or direction your message may take. Read their ideas, as well, to see different lines of approach.

Thursdays: Meet over lunch for about two hours. (If the meeting lasts longer than two hours, it usually becomes less productive.) Bring copies of possible illustrations, along with extra copies of what you have typed thus far. Your meeting place could be a church, home, or restaurant. But you may wish to rotate meeting at centrally located churches to allow immediate access to a copy machine, which is invaluable for distributing ideas without having to take the time to read every page each pastor brings. The copy machine can also save retyping or scanning the material and then e-mailing it to everyone.

Fridays: Follow up by faxing or e-mailing promising stories or articles that bubbled up in the meeting and have been requested by others. Group members may even e-mail their finished manuscripts to everyone else. Another set of ministerial eyes can reveal the need for significant additions, modifications, or deletions.

Remember the importance of meeting in person with the members of this group. Communicating by phone and e-mail may save time, but it rarely produces the prayer concerns or sharing of the heart that breeds much-needed camaraderie. So call two fellow preachers and form your own sermon-prep group today.

—DS

Group Publishing, Inc.
Attention: Product Development
P.O. Box 481
Loveland, CO 80539
Fax: (970) 679-4370

Evaluation for
60 Simple Secrets Every Pastor Should Know

Please help Group Publishing, Inc. continue to provide innovative and useful resources for ministry. Please take a moment to fill out this evaluation and mail or fax it to us. Thanks!

● ● ●

1. As a whole, this book has been (circle one)
not very helpful   very helpful

| 1 | 2 | 3 | 4 | 5 | 6 | 7 | 8 | 9 | 10 |

2. The best things about this book:

3. Ways this book could be improved:

4. Things I will change because of this book:

5. Other books I'd like to see Group publish in the future:

6. Would you be interested in field-testing future Group products and giving us your feedback? If so, please fill in the information below:

Name_____

Church Name _____

Denomination _____ Church Size _____

Church Address _____

City _____ State _____ ZIP _____

Church Phone _____

E-mail _____